365 things to DO in Ithaca NEW YORK

Complete Insider's Guide to All Things Ithaca

365 things to DO in Ithaca NEW YORK

Complete Insider's Guide to All Things Ithaca

BY LAUREL GUY

Schiffer Publishing Ltd
4880 Lower Valley Road • Atglen, PA 19310

Library of Congress Control Number: 2016946290

"Ithaka" was published in *C. P. Cavafy: Collected Poems*, ed. Edmund Keeley (Princeton University Press, 1975) and is reprinted with permission.

"Cascadilla Falls" was published in Collected Poems, 1951–1971, by A. R. Ammons (W. W. Norton & Company, 1972) and is reprinted with permission.

"What It's Like Living in Ithaca New York," by Dick Lourie, © Dick Lourie, 1978. Reprinted with permission of Hanging Loose Press.

Front Cover Photo Credits: Laurel Guy (Farmers Market, Stone VW, State Theatre, Clinton House, The Commons); Robyn Wishna (A. D. White Statue); Bill Warren (Dalai Lama); Jon Reis (Ithaca Festival Parade); Dede Hatch (Taughannock Falls); Cornell University Photography (Carl Sagan, Cornell at Night, Cornell Hockey, Cornell Crew); Dave Davies (Porchfest); Ithaca Beer (Ithaca Beer); Tommy Burns (The Burns Sisters); Cornell University Photography (Ithaca Shakespeare Company); Greek Peak (Greek Peak).

Back Cover Photo Credits: Laurel Guy (Gregar and Vicki Brous, Commons Market, Biking); Robyn Wishna (Rutabaga Curling); Cornell University Photography (Bailey Hall).
Cover Concept Design: Michael Rider, Rider Design
Production Design: DdF
Type set in Neutra Display/Miller Display/Latinaires

ISBN: 978-0-7643-5257-7
Printed in Hong Kong

Published by Schiffer Publishing, Ltd.
4880 Lower Valley Road
Atglen, PA 19310
Phone: (610) 593-1777; Fax: (610) 593-2002
E-mail: Info@schifferbooks.com
Web: www.schifferbooks.com

to

Ithaca,

with

Love

CONTENTS

INDEX

Introduction

Should I stay or should I go? I've lived in Ithaca for 35 years and I still ask myself this question every February. In the dead of winter when I'm digging my car out of a snow bank, it's hard to remember why I live here, yet by the time spring brings the heady fragrance of lilac bushes in full bloom, I've fallen back in love with Ithaca again. I call it seasonal amnesia. It is what keeps me here.

Thank goodness. Because it takes a very long time to get to know a place from the inside out. You need to stay for years to learn the shape of Ithaca, appreciate its peculiarities and quirks, the people, the history, the topography, and the seasons.

This book is a remembering of the reasons I have chosen to stay put. Each day, for a year, I wrote down one thing I loved about this place I call home. I began in the fall, when everything comes to fruition. Day by day, I take you through a year in the life of Ithaca—fall, winter, spring, summer. By the end of the book, we have circled back to where we started: autumn, the head of the year.

For me, Ithaca is not just one thing—it's everything! Waterfalls, the Farmers Market, chocolate, walking my dog Hugo in Upper Treman, local art, a great meal out with friends, DeWitt Mall, perfect clouds in a blue sky, Flat Rock, kindred spirits, picking blueberries, an amazing concert at the State Theatre, the smell of coffee brewing, fall colors, Taughannock Falls, people who can tap dance, Grassroots, fields of sunflowers, and Cayuga Lake. A giant gratitude list.

These 365 days are a small sample of this time and place. An average lifetime is 30,000 days. I hope you choose to stay awhile longer and discover the rest.

1 FIND THE STONE VW

Nowhere Else But Ithaca

The Stone VW Beetle is near Ringwood Road.

HINT

This hidden landmark *rocks*. It was built by Stephen Gibian in 1976.

2 GO APPLE PICKING

A Fall Favorite

It's harvest time. Farm-to-mouth, there's nothing like eating crisp, juicy New York State apples right off the tree. U-pick orchards include Little Tree Orchards, Indian Creek Farms, Grisamore Farms—or purchase freshly picked apples at the Cornell Orchard's store.

3 EAT AT THE STATE DINER

It's the Real Deal

This family owned old-style Greek diner is the real deal. Flawless service and a vast menu, including daily specials, breakfast any time, french fries with gravy, Tully burgers, Greek salad served with warm pita, perfect omelets, chocolate milkshakes, rice pudding, pie, and everything else under the Ithaca sun.

4 WIDE AWAKE BAKERY

Taste the Best Bread Ever

I am willing to be so bold as to say this bread might just change your life. Founded by visionary Stefan Senders, Wide Awake Bakery is local to the core. The bread is made from locally grown and milled grains and is delivered fresh, right out of the wood-fired oven. They bake up to 50 varieties of perfect loaves, including a German-style 100 percent rye, a mix-grain levain, and French-style country bread. Sign up for their CSA bread share. Members pick up bread once a week from a number of distribution sites in the Ithaca area. Oh, and they have one-day baking classes, too!

5 FRIENDS OF THE LIBRARY BOOK SALE

Go on the Quest for Hidden Treasures

This is the greatest used book sale on earth with over 250,000 books, audio books, CDs, DVDs, records, puzzles, and games. All of them super cheap. Our college town is full of academics and their donations are incredible—rarities, art books, first editions, and more. Ithacans love to read and people camp out overnight to get a good spot in line on opening day. They leave with their cars filled to the brim with books. The annual October and May sales benefit the Tompkins County Public Library.

TIP

The sale is a great place to volunteer and meet fellow bibliophiles.

6 GREATER ITHACA ART TRAIL

See Art Where It Happens

Connect with artists year-round by appointment or visit artist studios and watch works in progress on Open Studio weekends each October. Select studios are also open on the first Saturday of every month.

7 BEEBE LAKE

Enjoy the View

View Beebe Lake and Triphammer Falls from Sackett Footbridge at the heart of Cornell's campus. One of many breathtaking views and vistas around town.

CORNELL LEGEND

If a couple walks around the entire perimeter of Beebe Lake while holding hands, the two will get engaged.

8 CINEMAPOLIS

Check Out This Cool Arthouse Theater

See a movie at Cinemapolis, Ithaca's thriving nonprofit five-screen movie theater specializing in eclectic first-run indies and foreign films in a small setting downtown. Their addictive gourmet popcorn comes with real butter and a choice of toppings. You may not be able to resist their homemade cookies either. Become a member and earn points toward free tickets, popcorn, and more. (See entry 132.)

9 EAT LUNCH AT CAFE DEWITT

As Good As It Gets

Café DeWitt has gourmet omelets, sandwiches, soups, and salads with European flair. I love the Caesar sandwich but always check the blackboard for their daily specials. Dessert is hard to resist. A great place to people-watch: Lots of regulars—eating here will give you a flavor for the town. Open for breakfast and lunch only. Oh, and they have a superb Sunday brunch.

NOTE

Cash or checks only.

10 BECOME A FIREWALKER

Face Your Fears One Step at a Time

You'll walk through fire with Dr. Tony Simons, founder of Life Courage workshops. A powerful, life-changing experience. Between 10 and 30 people attend each of the monthly three-and-a-half-hour sessions.

11 INSECTAPALOOZA

Come See the Good, the Bad and the Bugly

Cornell's Department of Entomology's annual October one-day extravaganza celebrates insects with lots of kids' activities, games, and fun for everyone. Thousands of visitors enjoy butterfly zoos, cockroach races, cricket cookies, handfuls of maggots, and exotic insects from around the world. Learn to appreciate what insects do for us.

12 HAVE SUNDAY BRUNCH AT AMERICANA VINEYARDS

The Best Under-the-Radar Brunch Spot

The Crystal Lake Café at Americana Winery has amazing food made with local, seasonal ingredients. Everything, including the ketchup, is made from scratch. Afterward, wander to the tasting room in the rustic 1820s restored barn and try their wines. Free, live music every Friday evening and Sunday afternoon. Located in Interlaken, just 20 minutes or so from Ithaca.

13

HEAD TO ITHACA FARMERS MARKET *...of Course*

ON THE WATERFRONT

The Ithaca Farmers Market at Steamboat Landing is one of the best in the country, and Saturdays and Sundays, April through December, it is the place to be, our weekend ritual. You'll find a cornucopia of tasty foods, farm-fresh eggs, gorgeous produce and flowers, local meats, Finger Lakes wine, and handmade cheeses. Throw in a few artists, lots of great food vendors, and Cayuga Lake in the background. Is this what heaven is like? Visiting here will make you rethink your whole lifestyle.

NOTE

The Ithaca Farmers Market also happens on Tuesdays at DeWitt Park, Wednesdays at East Hill Plaza, and Thursday evenings at Steamboat Landing. (The Indoor Winter Market is January through March at the Greenstar Space.)

14 WILDER BRAIN COLLECTION

Raise Your IQ

Visit the showcase exhibiting eight brains from the Wilder Brain Collection in the psychology department on the second floor of Uris Hall at Cornell University. Established in 1889 by Dr. Burt Wilder, Cornell's first animal biologist, he is now better known as the fourth brain from the right. The collection includes the brain of Edward Rulloff, a murderer hanged in 1871 who possessed one of the largest brains on record, and suffragist Helen Hamilton Gardener, who donated her brain in 1925 to prove a woman's brain was in no way inferior to a man's.

15 SUNSET PARK

You Can See Forever

Sunset Park, a sweet postage stamp of a park in the Village of Cayuga Heights, has a bird's-eye view of the entire valley, the city lights of Ithaca, and a glimpse of Cayuga Lake, which always seems new, always surprises you. It's where Ithacans have gone for decades to catch the light at the end of the day and perhaps gain a little perspective. A place where many have come to pop the Question.... it's imbued with enough romance to guarantee the right answer.

16 ITHACA DOG PARK

Barking Up the Right Tree

The Ithaca Dog Park is a 4.8-acre, fenced, off-leash play area adjacent to Treman Marina. It's a clean and green dog heaven filled with tennis balls and doggie pools. Places to sit and shady areas make it an enjoyable spot for their owners, too. There's a separate, fenced area for petite canine friends.

17 EXPLORE THE CAYUGA LAKE WINE TRAIL

Sip the Wine, Savor the Day

Established in 1983, Cayuga Lake Wine Trail is America's first wine trail. It's a great drive on a crisp, fall day. Vineyards and wineries have been in this region since the 1700s, but it wasn't until 1976, when New York State passed the Farm Winery Act, that it was possible for grape growers to start small boutique wineries and sell directly to the public. Over the years, these small, family-run wineries have grown by leaps and bounds, bursting with idiosyncratic wines that have become internationally famous. Along Cayuga Lake are 16 wineries— including Lucas, Swedish Hill, Hosmer, King Ferry Winery, Knapp, and Sheldrake—a cidery, and four distilleries. It's a privilege to meet the vintners and hear their stories.

18 ¡VIVA! TAQUERIA

Taste Their Legendary "Ith-Mex"

This downtown corner eatery has the best handmade margaritas in town—the house margarita is Sauza Hornitos, Cointreau, and fresh lime juice. The menu includes healthy, delicious nachos, burritos, tacos, enchiladas, and more. Definitely try the chorizo fundido. Great ambience, outdoor seating, and reasonable prices makes this a fun go-to spot.

NOTE

Ith-Mex may not be Tex-Mex but it is still *muy bueno!*

19 VOLUNTEER AT THE CANCER RESOURCE CENTER

Make a Difference

The Cancer Resource Center of the Finger Lakes provides year-round comfort and assistance for those living with, and affected by, cancer. If you are looking for meaningful volunteer work, there are many ways you can give back. The staff will tailor their work to match your availability, skills, and interests. Volunteers are the heart of this organization—because no one should face cancer alone.

20 FIND THE YELLOW BRICK ROAD

There's No Place Like Home

State Street used to be paved with yellow bricks. L. Frank Baum, from Chittenango, New York, visited his future wife, Maud Gage, a student at Cornell, and legend has it Baum immortalized that yellow brick road later in *The Wizard of Oz*. While State Street was paved over and renamed Martin Luther King Jr. Blvd., the bricks remain. Some were reused in the 1930s to build this house. Find 1114 East Shore Drive, and click your heels together three times!

21 CONCERT PROMOTER, DAN SMALLS

Local Hero

Dan Smalls has reshaped the cultural landscape of our town—his memorable sold-out shows have kept the lights on at the State Theatre. His company, Dan Smalls Presents, books more than 75 shows a year in Ithaca, Rochester, and beyond. Dan produced his first concert as a Cornell sophomore and never looked back. Dan's got the knack for choosing the best mix of top musicians, shows, and comedy that draw crowds. He does it by taking care of the people who matter most: the bands and the fans. Follow Dan Smalls Presents and find out who's up next.

22 COLLEGETOWN BAGELS AND ITHACA BAKERY

Refuel at the Mothership

Collegetown Bagels and Ithaca Bakery. Two names, one family-owned business that started with a bagel and a dream in 1976, and today they have CTB/IB outposts all over town. It is where we go to jump-start our day. Organic, fair trade coffee, fresh-baked bagels, bialys and bread, outrageous sandwiches, wraps, soups, salads, and pastries. Their scones are the closest to the real thing on this side of the pond according to a British friend of mine.

23 TAUGHANNOCK FALLS OVERLOOK

Experience the Eighth Natural Wonder

Cascading beauty. Your worries will evaporate—at least while you're standing there. At 215 feet, Taughannock Falls is the highest single-drop waterfall east of the Rockies and is one of the most beautiful waterfalls in the world. Come here often, and in every season. In the winter the waterfall is frozen; in August it slows to just a trickle. There's also an easy hike to the base of the waterfall.

NOTE TO NEWCOMERS

Pronounce it "Tug-Ann-Nick." (See entry 304.)

24 TRICK-OR-TREAT IN FALL CREEK

It's Not Just for Kids

Halloween. It's fun for everyone, not just kids. The best place to go trick-or-treating is the Fall Creek neighborhood. Grab your ghouls and meet homeowners who stock up on vast amounts of candy for the hundreds of trick-or-treaters who come knocking on their doors. Don't worry, there's a separate bowl for vegan kids. (Hey, it's Ithaca!)

TIP

The house pictured is the Halloween Holy Grail: the best decorations and candy of all. Look for it on Tioga Street.

25

SEE A LIVE CONCERT AT THE *State Theatre*

A NIGHT TO REMEMBER

This 1928 downtown art deco theater is a magnificent 1,600-seat venue and presents a boatload of top acts—concerts, theater, dance, and comedy—over seventy concerts and shows each year. There are concessions available, including both wine and beer. This architectural gem has great acoustics and great seats.

TIP

Look up and see the twinkling stars on the ceiling.

26 WIZARDING WEEKEND

Bring Your Wand

Celebrate your love of all things Harry Potter and join thousands of muggles, wizards, and witches at the annual Halloween Wizarding Weekend in downtown Ithaca, when Press Bay Alley is magically tranformed into Daigon Alley. You'll finally get your acceptance letter to Hogwarts, play in a Quidditch match or wizard chess, and enjoy high-energy duels.

27 CORNELL BIG RED HOCKEY

Steeped in Tradition and Rivalry

Hockey at Cornell dates back more than a century. They've won the national championship twice and topped the ECAC a dozen times. Many players have gone on to star in the NHL. The Lynah Rink Faithful are loud and boisterous at home games, especially when Cornell plays Harvard—a fierce 98-year-old rivalry. If Cornell wins, the fans toss frozen fish on the ice and yell, "Sieve! Sieve! Sieve!" When you go to the game, remember to bring a newspaper with you. When the opposing team's line-up is announced, every Cornell fan pulls out their paper and starts waving it and chanting, "Boring! Boring!" Finally, all the newspapers are thrown out on the ice. Even the Zamboni driver gets into the spirit, dressing up in a different costume for every game.

28 TWO GOATS BREWING

Come for the Beer. Stay for the View.

A brewpub in a renovated 19th-century barn on Route 414 offers sweeping views of Seneca Lake and an excellent selection of fresh craft beer made from quality ingredients. Just one item on the menu: the best roast beef sandwich on the planet. No kidding. The chips and the pickle just look on in amazement. Great live music on the weekends. It's about a 35-minute drive from Ithaca. This is a gem of a place—folks, you need to go here.

29 FIND THE STONE EGG IN SAPSUCKER WOODS SANCTUARY

Cornell Lab of Ornithology

This remarkable cairn sculpture was built by internationally acclaimed environmental artist Andy Goldsworthy in 2008. It is tucked away in a quiet corner of Cornell's Sapsucker Woods. To find it, follow the Hoyt-Pileated Trail that begins across the road from the main entrance to the Cornell Lab of Ornithology. The stone egg sits on the right, a few minutes' walk down the trail.

BONUS

While you're there, visit the world-renowned Cornell Lab of Ornithology. It has a great visitor center with a bright, roomy observatory, interactive exhibits, seminars, bird guides, binoculars on loan, and more. Check out the magnificent 40-foot high, 3,000-square-foot Wall of Birds mural painted by Jane Kim, which features all 243 bird families.

30 REMEMBER CARL SAGAN

Celebrated Ithacan, Astronomer, and Visionary

No one has ever explained space as well as Sagan did. Besides being an astronomy professor at Cornell, he wrote more than a dozen books, worked on NASA robotic missions, and created the PBS series *Cosmos*. He was the most famous scientist in America and advocated for the greatest adventure of all: missions of discovery to worlds beyond our own. Find his old house at 900 Stewart Avenue. Perched on the edge of the gorge with incredible views of Ithaca Falls, the city lights, and Cayuga Lake, it was the perfect place to think cosmic thoughts. This mysterious bunker-like structure was built in 1890 as the meeting place for the Sphinx Head secret society and acquired by Sagan in the 1980s.

31 THE SAIGON KITCHEN

Try the Pho Ga

The Lam family creates fresh, made-from-scratch Vietnamese dishes. This is a lighter, fresher, insanely delicious version of Asian cuisine, and the dish leading the way is pho (pronounced with an upward, lilting glide: Fuh?) Try the Pho Ga (Vietnamese version of chicken soup—it will cure all that ails you); yummy spring rolls; crispy squid; and any of the traditional noodle dishes. Many vegetarian options. Reasonably priced. You'll be back.

32 WALK TO ITHACA FALLS

Right in the Heart of Ithaca

Listen to the roaring music of Ithaca Falls. I never get tired of it. It's a lovely surprise located in the downtown Fall Creek neighborhood, an easy walk, and truly magnificent. It's one of the first places I take visitors. In the autumn, this is the spot to go fly-fishing for brown trout and landlocked salmon. There are over 100 waterfalls in the area—many more to explore.

33 ROD SERLING

Get into "The Zone"

Watch an episode of *The Twilight Zone*. Rod Serling wrote episodes in an Airstream trailer just outside his family cottage on Cayuga Lake. The pioneering creator of one of the TV's best series lived here and taught at Ithaca College. Ithaca College is now the home of the Rod Serling Archives, an extensive collection of television scripts, movie screenplays, and films by Serling. The Bundy Museum in his hometown of Binghamton, New York, hosts a monthly symposium on his life and work.

34 PURITY ICE CREAM

Get a Taste of Ithaca History

Ithaca is the birthplace of the ice cream sundae. On April 3, 1892, Rev. John M. Scott ordered a bowl of vanilla cream at Platt & Colt Pharmacy. Owner Chester C. Platt topped it with cherry syrup and a candied cherry. It tasted so good, they felt obligated to name it, and the first "Cherry Sunday" was born. Purity Ice Cream has been an Ithaca staple since 1936, with dozens of delicious ice cream flavors and fountain creations. I always get Mocha Chip. (Vegan ice cream options available.) They also have scratch-baked pies and muffins. Eat dessert *first*. Then stay for lunch.

TIP

During the holiday season, it's all about the eggnog. Purity makes the best!

35 REIS TENNIS CENTER

Meet Your Match

Did you know you can play tennis 365 days a year in Ithaca? Reis Tennis Center is a six-indoor, six-outdoor court tennis complex. (They have squash courts, too.) Oh, you thought it was only for Cornell faculty, staff, and students? Nope! It's for everyone. Reasonable membership fees. Remember: love means nothing to a tennis player.

36 STEWART PARK

Sit at the Water's Edge

Watch the changing colors of the sky and Cayuga Lake, silhouetted by the iconic willow trees at Stewart Park. Aah! Close to downtown. A great place to relax, take a stroll, or play ultimate Frisbee. There are picnic pavilions, lots of green space, a duck pond, an old-fashioned merry-go-round, municipal golf course, and a bird sanctuary. It's also the home of the Cascadilla Boat Club. (See entry 100, 208, 351 and 354.)

37 THE STONECAT CAFE

Have an Unforgettable Meal

Chef Scott Signori and his wife, Jessica, fired up the smokers and started this seasonal restaurant in Hector, New York, in 1999. Farm-to-table food, great vibe, and phenomenal views of Seneca Lake. Pioneers of locally grown, organically produced food, their menu choices are always fresh and inspiring. They're famous for their garden-to-glass cocktails. Order a mojito and the bartender crushes up mint from the garden out back. Live music on weekends. On Route 414, the Seneca Lake Wine Trail, about 30 minutes from Ithaca. Strongly recommend reservations. Open May through November. Closed for the winter.

38 MARY MCDONNELL

From Ithaca to Hollywood

Mary McDonnell, Ithaca native, Oscar and Emmy-nominated actress, has an impressive body of work. Stay home. Take the day off and have a Mary McDonnell marathon! Catch her as Sharon Raydor in TNT's *Major Crimes* and *The Closer*, President Laura Roslin in *Battlestar Galactica*, as well as in *Dances with Wolves*, *Passion Fish*, *Grand Canyon*, *Sneakers*, *Independence Day*, and more. After you've watched her fight crime, fall in love, and save the world, everything will look a little bit brighter and you'll be ready to face tomorrow.

39 DISCOVER THE HORSEFLIES

Be Transported

The legendary Horseflies are a classic string band but with synth and percussion, creating a hypnotic and intense dance groove. Since 1981, they've toured the US, Canada, and Europe, blowing people's minds with their innovative sound. The Flies have put out eight albums and made some film scores. Listen to *Until the Ocean* or *Gravity Dance*, and go see them live.

40 DEWITT PARK

Conjure Up the Past

Go to Dewitt Park, in the very center of town, close your eyes, and imagine it as it was long ago, when it was inhabited by Native Americans, the Lamoka, from 3000 BC. This park was sacred land, a crossroads: many Native American trails intersected near what is now the First Presbyterian Church. There's history and spirit in this area. Can you feel it? Look around and see as it is now—it's still a crossroads in our life today. The spirit remains.

41 RASA SPA

Indulge in a Spa Day

Pamper yourself at Rasa Spa. Sip tea in a luxurious robe in the tranquility room while you wait for your treatment. Massage and bodywork, Reiki, reflexology, acupuncture, facials, waxing, meditation, yoga, and aromatherapy are among the treatments offered. It's a decadent gift to yourself —a mini vacation. Hey, you deserve it. Take advantage of the sauna, too. Rasa's amenities and practitioners are first class.

42 GET SOME GIMME!

A Coffee Lover's Paradise

Best cuppa in town. Urban chic. Locally roasted beans. Gimme! has been voted one of the best coffee places in New York State. It's made by professional baristas who take the art of coffee-making seriously, creating perfect espresso and latte art every single time. You'll find a good selection of teas and pastries, too. Slowly read the newspaper, check your email, and stay as long as you like.

43 CONTRA DANCING

Give It a Whirl

Ithaca has a thriving contra dance community including Tompkins County Country Dancers and Hands Four Dancers. It's a welcoming, joyous style of dance, and there's always live music. Jump right in! You start dancing with the person across from you, and subsequent partners send you down the line. By the time the song ends, you've danced with everyone.

44 DOROTHY COTTON

Civil Rights Pioneer

A charismatic Ithaca icon, lifelong activist, and one of the pioneers of the civil rights movement, Dr. Dorothy Cotton worked closely with Dr. Martin Luther King. In the 1960s, Dr. Cotton was the education director and highest-ranking woman in the Southern Christian Leadership Conference. In 1982, Dr. Cotton accepted a position at Cornell as director of student activities. In the 1990s, she traveled widely, leading seminars and workshops on leadership and social change. She received a National Freedom Award in 2010. Read her superb book, *If Your Back's Not Bent*—she gives her perspective on the freedom struggle led by Dr. King. Learn more at the Dorothy Cotton Institute of Cornell University, which was founded as a tribute to her legacy of social change.

45 THE PORTS OF NEW YORK

A Must-Stop on the Cayuga Inlet

You'll be instantly transported to France when you walk in the door. *Fantastique!* The owner and winemaker, Frédéric Bouché, comes from a long line of winemakers. You'll taste two gorgeous Meleau port wines in fine glassware. No plastic here! Imagine sitting near a roaring fire on a snowy evening sipping a glass of port. The thought of it almost—almost—makes me like winter.

The Dalai Lama's Monastery Is Here

For 25 years, this Victorian home at 412 N. Aurora St. housed Namgyal Monastery—the North American Seat of His Holiness the 14th Dalai Lama and the only branch of his monastery outside India. It is open to all. The monastery has now moved to Du Khor Choe Ling, an inspiring 28-acre campus designed according to traditional Tibetan architecture, just three miles from downtown Ithaca on Route 96B. The resident monks offer authentic teachings of Tibetan Buddhism, weekly meditation, and many cultural events open to the public. The Dalai Lama's message of kindness and compassion is for all of us, regardless of religious affiliation.

47

JOHNSON MUSEUM *of Art*

EXPERIENCE THE PERFECT SMALL MUSEUM

Cornell University's Herbert F. Johnson Museum of Art has some of the finest collections in New York State. The concrete and glass building designed by I. M. Pei is a work of art itself. The interplay of galleries and outdoor spaces frames the art perfectly. It's on a knoll high above Cayuga's waters, in the exact spot where Ezra Cornell chose the site for his university. Musts: The spectacular fifth-floor, 360-degree view of Cornell, Ithaca, and Cayuga Lake; the new Cosmos light installation at the second-floor sculpture court; and before you leave, clap your hands in the exterior alcove of the south side of building and hear the echo!

48 CAN YOU FIND ITHACA'S SWAN?

An Unsolved Mystery

The legend of Ithaca's swan. See it for yourself. Drive at night on Route 96B down South Hill towards Ithaca. Look to the left after you pass Ithaca College and just before you reach Rogan's Corner, you will see the elusive swan lighting up West Hill. Is it an accidental pattern of the city lights or a planned design? Hmmm, a mystery.

49 SHOULD YOU GET GLOVES OR MITTENS?

The Eternal Winter Dilemma

Go on a quest to find the perfect pair of winter gloves. Or should you get mittens? Smart gloves keep your hands warm, and you can use your touchscreen phone at the same time. *Or* get Cece & Lulu's cozy warm mittens made locally from upcycled sweaters—available at 15 Steps on the Commons. Hugo recommends you get *both*!

BONUS

They will cheer you up through the long, gray winter.

50 EAT AT AGAVA RESTAURANT

Great Atmosphere, Splendid Seasonal Menu

It's got the buzz. A Southwest-inspired restaurant featuring a wood-fired oven, seasonal menu, and locally sourced ingredients. The bar has agave flights, tasty beers, signature cocktails, and a great wine list. Try their wood-fired flatbread pizzas, fish tacos, burgers, and wings. Outdoor seating on the covered patio. Live music on weekends. It's the perfect destination for a casual meal or a festive celebration.

51 GO TO WEGMANS

Oh, You're Already There?

But, of course! It's not an exaggeration to say Wegmans is the greatest supermarket the world will ever know. This family owned 100-year-old grocery store chain based out of Rochester, New York, was recently named the best in the country in a consumer survey. You'll find a bakery, deli, pizzeria, French patisserie, cheese shop, caterer, butcher, sushi counter, vegetarian bar, international foods, health food, coffee shop, florist, pharmacy, take-out food, sit-down restaurant, home goods store, and oh, some groceries, too. If only they had apartments upstairs, then we would never have to leave. Danny Wegman, are you listening?

52 CORNELL'S CREATIVE WRITING READING SERIES

Be Inspired by Your Favorite Authors

Cornell's Creative Writing Department hosts the Barbara and David Zalaznick Reading Series, which has featured Billy Collins, Junot Diaz, Salman Rushdie, and Margaret Atwood among others. Every semester, several renowned and prize-winning authors visit the campus and their readings are free and open to the public.

NOTE

Some of the most distinguished writers in American letters have taught or studied at Cornell including E. B. White, Kurt Vonnegut, Thomas Pynchon, and Toni Morrison.

53 BUY LOCAL FIRST

Keep It Up-Close and Personal

Ithacans are independent thinkers and set our own trends. We like to buy what is locally grown, locally made in our own backyard. Although many of the chain stores have now moved to town, Ithacans prefer to support people we know personally—talented artisans and small business owners, which keeps dollars in the local economy and builds a thriving community.

54 FIRST FRIDAY GALLERY NIGHT

Go Gallery Hopping

One of our most popular events is a monthly walkable tour of more than 20 downtown Ithaca galleries and art houses. Free and open to the public on the first Friday of every month from 5 to 8 p.m. More than 1,000 artists make their home in Tompkins County. Gallery Night allows you to see a different slice each month, bringing people together to experience art in a relaxed way.

55 ITHACA ALTERNATIVE GIFT FAIR

Avoid the Stress of Holiday Shopping

Are you like me at holiday time? Do you procrastinate? Realize you waited too long to buy and send gifts? Rush out and buy gifts no one actually wants or needs? Bah, Humbug! Go to Ithaca Alternative Gift Fair instead. An inspired way to honor friends and relatives with donations to causes and charities they are passionate about. Gifts for Good will never be forgotten, thrown out, or given away.

56 ASIA CUISINE

Craving Korean Food?

Asia Cuisine on Aurora Street. OMG, the food is so good. Huge menu. Nice variety of Korean, Japanese, and Chinese cuisine. Kimchi, bibim bop, tofu bokkum, sushi, General Tso's chicken, homemade noodles and more—great food at an inexpensive price. This tiny place will become your favorite lunch or dinner spot.

57 THE BOARDMAN HOUSE

Where Ithaca College Got Its Start

"We acted our hearts out, made music in the park, filled the church choirs with wonderful voices, and generally added life to the culture in Ithaca." W. Grant Egbert, an accomplished violinist, founded the Ithaca Conservatory of Music in 1892, setting it up in four rooms of a home at 403 E. Seneca Street. Classrooms and dorms were established in many downtown buildings. In 1910, the Boardman House in DeWitt Park became the heart of Ithaca College until they moved to their new campus on South Hill in the 1960s. Tens of thousands of students and 125 years later, Ithaca College has become one of the top-ranked colleges in the country.

58 DONNA THE BUFFALO

Herd of 'em?

Another local band you need to know. Their original roots music is buoyant and beautiful, infused with elements of Cajun, rock, folk, reggae, and country. DtB is one of the founding and host bands of the annual Finger Lakes Grassroots Festival of Music and Dance, nominated one of *USA Today*'s top 10 outdoor music festivals. (See entry 299.)

59 SAGE CHAPEL CHRISTMAS VESPERS

Hear Choirs of Angels

Don't miss Cornell's Sage Chapel annual candlelit Christmas Vespers, held the first week in December. It is the absolute best. Wondrous performances from the Cornell Choir and Glee Club—they sound like angels – and traditional readings and hymns. While you're there, take a closer look at the glittering mosaics and the Tiffany windows. Sage Chapel is a nondenominational chapel that beautifully blends spirituality with learning, and is the final resting place for Cornell's founders Ezra Cornell, A. D. White, and their wives.

60 GREEK PEAK SKI RESORT

Hit the Slopes

A varied terrain suitable for skiers and boarders of all skill levels, Greek Peak Ski Resort, just 20 miles or so from Ithaca in Cortland, features terrain parks and a half pipe, cross-country skiing, snowshoeing, and night skiing. Did you know there's an Adventure Center with a Mountain Coaster, four tandem zip lines, and a snow-tubing center? Hope Lake Lodge at Greek Peak includes three restaurants, a spa, fitness center, and indoor waterpark.

61 TRAMPOLINE

Have We Got a Story for You

Storytelling. It's at the core of all that makes us human. Trampoline is a *Moth*-like monthly storytelling competition held at Lot 10 Bar and Lounge on S. Cayuga Street, on the second Thursday of the month, 7 to 9 p.m. Participants have five minutes to tell an original story based loosely on a predetermined theme. Founded by local novelist Bob Proehl, Trampoline engages the audience like few other events can. You'll feel the electricity as you listen to spellbinding stories and root for your favorites.

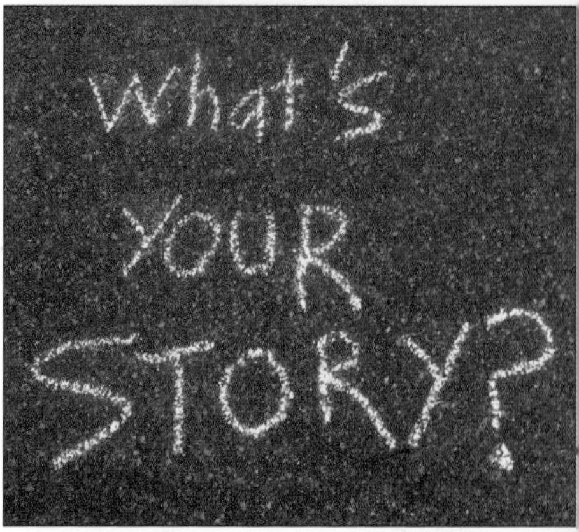

62 TOMPKINS COUNTY PUBLIC LIBRARY

Get Your Library Card

The Tompkins County Public Library was founded in 1864 by Ezra Cornell. Our fabulous library is at the heart of community life. It has annual circulation of 263,000 items—books, magazines, videos, music CDs—and offers free Internet, author readings, story time, music, art exhibits, many cultural events, and the annual Community Read.

63 SPCA OF TOMPKINS COUNTY

How You Can Help

There are many ways to get involved with our local SPCA. It is a no-kill shelter, and the nation's first "green" animal shelter—the facility is good for people, good for animals, and good for the planet. Volunteer if you love animals and can give them one shift per week. They promise good feelings and fun.

DONATE

Your gift will provide food, shelter, and medical care.

ADOPT

Is it time you found your forever friend?

64

MOOSEWOOD *Restaurant*

VISIT VEGGIE MECCA

It is not completely clear who coined the word "vegetarian." But we know who put it on the map. The member-owners of Ithaca's world-famous Moosewood Restaurant bring love, good cooking, and good humor to the table. Named one of the "13 most influential restaurants of the 20th century" by Bon Appétit magazine. The Moosewood Collective has written 13 best-selling cookbooks, sharing their recipes with people all over the world.

65 ITHACA ICE FESTIVAL AND CHOWDER COOK-OFF

Have Fun at This Frosty Extravaganza

The tastiest part of Downtown Ithaca's Ice Festival in December is the annual Chowder Cook-off, with 20 restaurants competing for the coveted Chowder Cup. While tasting the warm winter chowders, enjoy Ithaca Ice Wars—ice carvers compete in three live competitions to win the prize money. Don't miss the Ice Bar—an outdoor bar made entirely of ice, serving beer, wine, and cocoa. The walkable tour of finished ice sculptures will last as long as our winter weather cooperates.

66 ITHACA BALLET'S ANNUAL *NUTCRACKER*

Put Down the Eggnog

You have a ballet to attend. Treat your lovelies to Ithaca Ballet's annual *Nutcracker* at the State Theatre, that shimmering spectacle of holiday cheer. For many children, following Clara on her journey to the Land of Sweets is their first experience with dance. Ithaca Ballet is Upstate New York's only repertory company. It has trained more than 2,000 young people in the art of dance, and performs four productions a year in the State Theatre.

67 NORTHSTAR HOUSE

Come On In and Stay Awhile

Everybody knows your name at this cozy neighborhood pub in Fall Creek. It's a good mix of old-school bistro and modern gourmet. It has an extensive list of beers, spirits, and wines, with an eclectic menu and delectable Sunday brunch. Legit vegan options. Outdoor dining and beer garden. My favorite items are the Jerked Tofu Wings, Kangaroo Dip (OMG!!), and the burgers. Oh, and a different mac-n-cheese every day. Seriously. Words cannot do it justice, but let me say this: If I were on death row and choosing my final meal, Northstar's mac-n-cheese would be it.

68 A WORD ABOUT THE WEATHER

Fifty Shades of Gray

Juneau, Seattle, and Cleveland get less sunshine. Syracuse, Buffalo, and Rochester get far more snow. Some days you do have to settle for clouds. Yet even when the sky is the texture and color of liquid concrete, there is often that moment late in the day, when the sun finally dips below the ceiling of gray and blazes up like an answer to a question you didn't even know you were asking. "There. There it is," I say. "Now we can go home."

69 BROWSE AT BUFFALO STREET BOOKS

Your Very Own Bookstore

Once upon a time, Ithaca had 12 independent bookstores, and then a funny thing happened: the Internet. Suddenly we were down to just one independent bookstore and it was going to close. No. Say it ain't so! So, a place for readers was reborn—Buffalo Street Books is our lively, community-owned, cooperative bookstore. Hundreds of owners. Thousands of books. One great bookstore. What a novel idea. And, we all lived happily ever after.

70 THE CLAY SCHOOL OF ITHACA

Fire Up Your Imagination

The Clay School, founded by potter Julia e. Dean, is a hands-on teaching studio for community members of all ages to work with clay and learn alongside emerging and professional potters. Wheel-throwing, hand-building, surface decoration, and functional work. Extended classes, weekend, and one-day workshops. Use your imagination, and get your hands dirty.

71 THE INTERNATIONAL RUTABAGA CURLING CHAMPIONSHIP

All You Need Is a Rutabaga and a Dream

This annual event takes place at high noon at the Ithaca Farmers Market on the last day of the outdoor market season. December has arrived, and the temperatures are well below freezing. There's typically a dusting of snow and a biting wind coming off the lake. But Ithacans are hardy folk and they are dressed for the occasion. The top three contestants in the championship round are awarded gold, silver, and bronze medals, along with eternal glory, honor, and fame. Highlights include Handel's "Rutabaga Chorus" by the Vociferous Cruciferous chorus.

72 ATLAS BOWL

Eat, Drink, Bowl

Atlas Bowl in Trumansburg is a great place to go with a group of friends. This restaurant has fun, retro vibe, and seven bowling lanes. Not your father's bowling alley! It's in a league of its own. There's a full bar with craft choices, and fresh, delicious pub-style food with great tacos and burgers, loaded tater tots, and lots of vegetarian options.

73 WALK A WINTER WONDERLAND

Christmas Lights at Night

Enjoy the sparkly glow of Christmas lights on an evening stroll through the peaceful Fall Creek neighborhood. It's a beautiful time to experience Ithaca, tucked in for the night in a blanket of snow.

74 RUNNING TO PLACES THEATRE COMPANY

Go See *A Christmas Carol*

Don't be a Scrooge. See Running to Places (R2P) perform Charles Dickens's *A Christmas Carol*. Make this one of your annual traditions. This musical journey through past, present, and future is performed at the State Theatre. R2P, Ithaca's premier youth theater company, is made up of about 150 passionate and dedicated youths in grades six to 12 who come together to make quality theatre. Check out their season.

Embrace the First Big Snow

Back in the 1880s an anthropologist noted that the Inuit people in Canada had many words for describing snow: *aqilokoq* for "softly falling snow" and *piegnartoq* for "the snow [that is] good for driving sled." Describing Ithaca's snow one morning:: "snow slightly crunchy on top," "snow sparkling like diamonds," "snow [that is] good for making snow angels," "snow [that is] good for driving cars—all the roads are plowed, yay!"

76 JENNIFER ENGEL

The Perfect Gift Guide

Are you stuck looking for an appropriate present? When I can't think what to give, I go see Jennifer Engel at Cat's Pajamas in DeWitt Mall. For more than 30 years, Cat's Pajamas has been Ithaca's original general store for kids, and kids at heart. Trendy jewelry, lizard flashlights, and talking parrot pens. Noise makers, sparkly things, tiaras! Quality baby clothes. The softest stuffed animals. Toys and games. Jennifer spreads good cheer in all seasons.

77 THE GLENWOOD PINES

Order the Pinesburger

Some things don't change. This old-time tavern is not just a restaurant, it is *the* Ithaca place to be. Beyond the great atmosphere are the Pinesburger (this handmade burger right off the grill is the best in Ithaca), fresh haddock fish fry, a beautiful view of Cayuga Lake, and the bowling machine.

78 DELIGHT IN THE CITY LIGHTS AT NIGHT

Like Stars on the Ground

The silver lining of winter's shorter days? The longer we have to admire the night views of this jewel we call home.

79 GIVE IT UP FOR THE BURNS SISTERS

One of Ithaca's Greatest Natural Resources

The Burns Sisters have sung their hearts out for us. We have loved them right back, through thick and thin, listening to their unforgettable harmonies on 14 albums and at countless concerts and fundraisers. Five sisters: Sheila, Marie, Annie, Jeannie, and Terry come from a family of 12 children—seven brothers—raised in Binghamton, New York. Mom was an opera singer, and they grew up singing. The Burns Sisters have performed and recorded in various sibling constellations and currently consist of Annie and Marie. Jeannie is writing and performing with Andrew Hardin. Terry is writing and performing with her husband, Ron Kristy.

80 ITHACA COLLEGE TOWERS

Watch the New Year Arrive

The landmark Ithaca College Towers light up South Hill with the last two digits of the year during the final week of December. At the stroke of midnight on December 31, the 14-story-high numbers change. It's Ithaca's artful version of the Times Square ball drop and has been a tradition since 1965. Many local New Year's Eve parties are planned around a good view of the changing year.

81 THE MUSEUM OF THE EARTH

Take a Journey through 4.5 Billion Years

Walk inside a glacier and hear the ice cracking at the cool and kid-friendly Museum of the Earth, the natural history museum of the Paleontological Research Institution. A glacier, the main character of our story, carved out our long, deep lakes and steep-walled gorges more than 20,000 years ago. Hands-on exhibits for even the smallest paleontologists. Check out dinosaurs and dig for fossils. through time. While you're there, take a journey through time and walk past an entire eon, 550 million years, depicted in the stunning masterpiece *Rock of Ages, Sands of Time* by local artist Barbara Page. Contemplate the massive Hyde Park mastodon. (See entry 250.)

82 GREENSTAR NATURAL FOODS CO-OP MARKET

You Belong Here

GreenStar is essential for Ithaca living. Come here to get local flavor and a real sense of community. Of course, there are thousands of organic, natural, fair trade, and local products. You can buy many items in bulk including eggs, spices, sugar, flour, grains, maple syrup, fresh local tofu by the block, and much more. I love their expansive wellness department with a knowledgeable staff to guide you. Look into their list of cooking, health, and wellness classes, too. Three locations.

83 MERCATO BAR & KITCHEN

The Perfect "Date Night" Restaurant

Mercato is a small, upscale restaurant where the food and atmosphere are worth every penny. You'll feel like you stepped into a trattoria in Bologna or Firenze. Handmade pastas—perfect gnocchi that is light and delicate. Exceptional wines and innovative cocktails (try the Ithaca 37). No reservations.

84 ACK! IT'S TEN BELOW

Time to Escape to the Beach

In the dead of winter there's nothing sweeter than dreaming of a beach escape. In February 2015, Ithaca Tourism posted a picture of a beach on its homepage and said, "Don't come here, go to Florida!" Of course, it went viral and made the national news. That's what Ithacans do in the winter—we either escape to the beach or dream of it. It's how we survive. The sun. The sound of the waves. The smell of warm salt air. Your shoulders relax as you realize how much your body has been braced against the cold. Imagine your first walk on the beach. Bare feet. Warm sand. Fresh seafood. Consider the possibilities. Check for cheap flights. *Ooops!* It's time to leave for work, and the driveway still needs to be shoveled. Back to reality.

85 CAYUGA BIRD CLUB

Join the Christmas Bird Count

Birding can turn every walk into a treasure hunt. On New Year's Day, the Cayuga Bird Club participates in the annual Christmas Bird Count—the nation's longest-running citizen science bird project. This season, birdwatchers may enjoy sightings of snowy owls. The Christmas Bird Count is an ideal way to introduce kids to birding. The Cayuga Bird Club offers many beginner bird walks at Sapsucker Woods, Cornell Lab of Ornithology. Seek them out.

A must-read for All Ithacans

A perfect poem for a New Year's Day,
or for any new day.

Ithaka

As you set out for Ithaka
hope your road is a long one,
full of adventure, full of discovery.
Laistrygonians, Cyclops,
angry Poseidon – don't be afraid of them;
you'll never find things like that on your way
as long as you keep your thoughts raised high,
as long as a rare excitement
stirs your spirit and your body.
Laistrygonians, Cyclops,
wild Poseidon – you won't encounter them
unless you bring them along inside your soul,
unless your soul sets them up in front of you.

Hope your road is a long one.
May there be many summer mornings when,
with what pleasure, what joy,
you enter harbors you're seeing for the first time;
may you stop at Phoenician trading stations
to buy fine things,
mother of pearl and coral, amber and ebony,
sensual perfumes as you can;
and may you visit many Egyptian cities
to learn and go on learning from their scholars.

Keep Ithaka in your mind.
Arriving there is what you're destined for.
But don't hurry the journey at all.
Better if it lasts for years,
so you're old by the time you reach the island,
wealthy with all you've gained along the way,
not expecting Ithaka to make you rich.

Ithaka gave you the marvelous journey.
Without her you wouldn't have set out.
She has nothing left to give you now.

And if you find her poor, Ithaka won't have fooled you.
Wise as you will have become, so full of experience,
You'll have understood by then what these Ithakas
mean.

87 CARGILL SALT MINE

Journey to the Center of the Lake

The Cargill Salt Mine in Lansing is like a journey to another planet. It is 2,300 feet under the center of Cayuga Lake, with temperatures in the 70s year-round. It is the deepest rock salt mine in North America—remnants of a sea that dried up 400 million years ago. Although it is not open to the public, just knowing there are salt mine workers underneath the lake staggers the imagination. They process approximately two million tons of road salt every year.

88 WALK ACROSS COLLEGE AVENUE BRIDGE

A "Gorges" View

You look down on the rushing white current of the waterfall below. From early on, the specter of suicide haunted Ithaca's gorges. Cornell's suicide rate is historically the same as other colleges and universities, yet its rate of suicide by jumping is dramatically higher. Cornell recently installed nets on seven bridges on or near campus as a deterrent.

89 LINDSETH CLIMBING WALL

Onward and Upward

We appreciate the extra breathing room between semesters when the students leave. This is a good time for townies to explore campus and Collegetown. Try out the Lindseth Climbing Wall. It is the largest indoor natural rock-climbing wall in North America. Located in Bartels Hall on the Cornell University campus, it is 160 feet wide by 30 feet high: 4,800 square feet of climbing surface. Rock-climbing is a full body workout and will feed your craving for adventure. It's a rush! Good for participants of any age or ability level.

| 90 SAY HELLO TO JACK GOLDMAN

The Bookery

Jack is a quiet twinkly presence, and is well known for his contributions to local literature and political activism. Before opening The Bookery in 1975, he devoted several years to opposing the Vietnam War and doing community organizing. When you walk into The Bookery, you'll feel as though you've entered Jack's personal library, which is filled with literary treasures—more than 35,000 volumes of used and rare books. You'll love perusing here. Jack writes luminous haiku poems that capture a single moment. Pictured is one he wrote on a day I visited.

| 91 COMMUNITY SCHOOL OF MUSIC AND ART

Take a Creative Class

Do you have a passion or hobby you've always wanted to pursue? The Community School of Music and Arts (CSMA) provides a diverse array of quality classes for kids and adults, including ballet, hip-hop, belly dancing, tap dance, drawing, painting, watercolor, banjo, cello, clarinet, guitar, percussion, piano, recorder, saxophone, viola, violin, voice, and more. (See entry 305.)

92 WINTER VILLAGE BLUEGRASS FESTIVAL

Cure Your Cabin Fever

It's winter; it's cold, it's dark, and you want to scream. Don't despair. The Winter Village Bluegrass Festival in January will warm you up with the some of the best bluegrass pickers, lightning fast tempos, and vocal harmonies around. Enjoy guitar, fiddle, banjo, and a little southern twang.

93 RED FEET WINE MARKET & SPIRIT PROVISIONS

Uncork New Wines

They specialize in uncommon wines, little gems and spirits from around the world. Check out their Thursday tastings called "Hang Time," where they feature different wines based on a theme. Enjoy some crusty bread, cheese, and olives to munch on while tasting. Knowledgeable staff, fun crowd, and a good time! You'll leave knowing a lot more about wine than when you arrived.

94 ISLAND HEALTH AND FITNESS

Join the Gym

Winter is the perfect time to get started. Island Health and Fitness is a state-of-the-art gym. The huge wall of windows overlooking Cayuga Inlet provides a fantastic view while you're working out. There's also a great pool, and they have every machine you can think of and lots of classes. Go!

95 SEASONAL AMNESIA

Forgetting Is a Choice

Seasonal amnesia is when in the midst of summer, you simply cannot remember winter. And vice versa. This is the key. We couldn't live here without it. It makes the change of season an unexpected surprise. Every. Single. Time.

96 GO TO MAXIE'S SUPPER CLUB AND OYSTER BAR

A Little Down-Home Southern Comfort

Here are 10 reasons y'all need to go to Maxie's Supper Club: 1. Jambalaya 2. Shrimp and grits 3. Half-priced raw oysters, 4–6 p.m. 4. Perfect rack of ribs 5. Pan-fried catfish 6. Po' boys 7. Chicken-fried Tuesdays 8. Live music Sundays and Tuesdays 9. Fried green tomatoes 10. Festive NOLA vibe—Mardi Gras beads.

97 THE FINGER LAKES

Do You Know All Their Names?

The Iroquois tribes believed the Finger Lakes were formed when the Great Spirit laid his hands on the land. They are named: Conesus (Always Beautiful), Hemlock (the only lake not named by the tribes), Canadice (Long Lake), Honeoye (Finger Lying), Canandaigua (Chosen Spot), Keuka (Canoe Landing), Seneca (Place of the Stone), Cayuga (Boat Landing), Owasco (Floating Bridge), Skaneateles (Long Lake), and Otisco (Waters Dried Away).

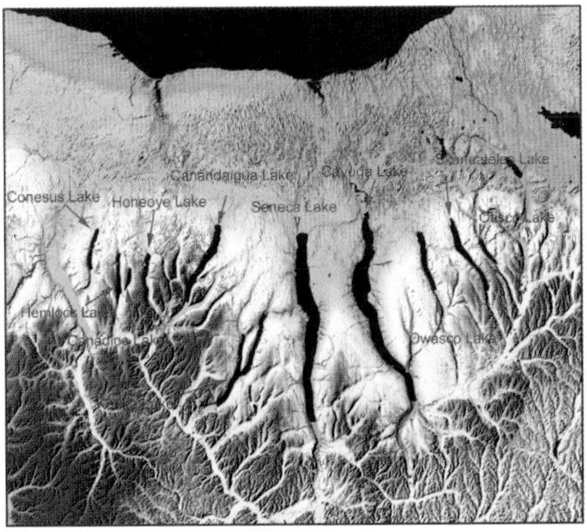

98 SIMPLIFY YOUR LIFE

Reduce, Reuse, Recycle

Live William Morris's maxim: "Have nothing in your house you do not know to be useful or believe to be beautiful." Don't just clean your house. Do a master cleanse, using the three Rs of Ithaca—reduce, reuse, and recycle. Mimi's Attic will sell one item or a truckload on consignment. Finger Lakes Reuse Center accepts used furniture, household goods, electronics, and building materials. Donations are tax deductible. Tompkins County Solid Waste and Recycling has drop-off areas for trash and recycling.

99 THE CORNING MUSEUM OF GLASS

Take a Drive to Corning, NY

The Corning Museum of Glass (CMOG) is extraordinary, especially the new contemporary Art & Design Wing—a $64 million, 100,000 square-foot, light-gathering glass masterpiece. They have the world's largest glass collection—50,000 objects representing 3,500 years of glass and glass-making. CMOG also offers classes in their studio and they have a glass camp for kids. Year-round exhibitions focus on the art, science, and history of glass. Live glass-making demos. Just about a 45-minute drive from Ithaca.

100 WHARTON BROTHERS STUDIO

Did You Know They Made Movies Here?

More than 100 years ago, Ithaca was the original Movie Capital of the World. The Wharton Brothers set up their movie studio at Stewart Park and made some of the biggest films of the silent movie era. Excitement gripped the town. Locals enthusiastically played extras. Lavishly dressed movie stars strolled downtown and drove flashy cars. A huge crowd gathered to watch the big stunt for a 1914 thriller: a trolley car careening off the bridge onto the rocks below.

NOTE

The popular term "cliffhanger," referring to a suspenseful plot technique designed to keep the audience wanting more, originated here. The Wharton Brothers filmed a series, *The Exploits of Elaine*, featuring a female protagonist who was left in grave danger at the end of each episode, compelling the audience to come back the following week to find out if and how she escaped. One episode concluded with the protagonist literally hanging off the edge of a cliff, coining the popular phrase. (See entry 36.) Visit the online Wharton Studio Museum to learn more.

101 ITHACA FESTIVAL MURAL

Come See What Our Community Looks Like

Five hundred people of all ages stopped to paint a tile at the 1997 Ithaca Festival. Five hundred different moments. The finished mural is a vision of what we create together as a community. It's a permanent installation in Dewitt Mall near the entrance to the Moosewood Restaurant. Stop by to see it.

102 LOAVES AND FISHES

They Need You

Loaves and Fishes began with a single pot of soup in 1983. Last year they served more than 37,000 meals. It's not a typical soup kitchen. It's a community. "A lot of our guests are completely alone. Loaves & Fishes becomes their community, and when they need help, they turn to us," said Christina Culver, the director. It was voted the best place to volunteer in the *Ithaca Times* Best of Ithaca poll. It's a happy atmosphere and no matter what your task, your presence and willingness to be open and interact with others is more than enough to impact someone's life.

103 ALICE MUHLBACK

Discover Her Spirit & Kitsch

Whimsical. Alice Muhlback is a much-loved artist, cartoonist, and graphic designer. Hang around Ithaca long enough and you'll see her iconic raven on t-shirts, coffee mugs, and bumper stickers. Alice's view of the world is inspiring and quirky, and her affordable art is available online at her site Spirit and Kitsch, at the Ithaca Farmers Market, and at Ithacamade in the DeWitt Mall.

104 GO CROSS-COUNTRY SKIING

Hammond Hill State Forest

Glide back to nature through pristine meadows and rolling hills. Go cross-country skiing at Hammond Hill State Forest. Nineteen miles of marked trails suitable for skiing, hiking, mountain biking, and horseback riding.

105 ITHACA COFFEE COMPANY

A Great Place to Unwind

There's a vibrant coffee culture brewing in Ithaca. The Ithaca Coffee Company is another place where you can recharge. They roast coffee beans to perfection and their two locations focus on excellent coffee and confections as well as a huge selection of craft beers, beer-making supplies, and gourmet food.

106 GOLA OSTERIA

When You Find It, You'll Love It

Now *that's* Italian! Fresh, fresh pasta is made on site. Gnocci, pumpkin ravioli, squid ink pasta with clams, grilled octopus, perfect porchetta, housemade focaccia, and more. Save room for dessert if you can; try the chocolate budino with hazelnuts.

NOTE

The location inside the Quarry Arms is a little obscure—somewhat confusing to find but so worth the effort.

107 FUERTES OBSERVATORY

Study the Stars

To boldly go! Experience the sense of wonder a clear night and billions of stars can give. Visit the Fuertes Observatory. Public viewing nights are clear Fridays, 9 p.m. to midnight. Organized by the Cornell Astronomical Society.

108 DON'T MISS DJUG DJANGO AT LOT 10

Ithaca's Best-Kept Secret

Djug Django plays classic gypsy swing by Django Reinhardt, originals by Dave Davies, and the best of the blues at Lot 10 Bar and Lounge every Wednesday from 6 to 9 p.m. Magic happens here—you'll be transported to a 1920s speakeasy. These are some of Ithaca's best musicians—long-time professional players with national reputations. No cover. No minimum. An exuberant scene with food, wine, and room for dancing. Shhh!

109 THE QUAKER PEACEFUL PROTEST

Cheer Them On

Watch for the Quakers at the bottom of East State Street during rush hour on Thursdays, and give them a wave! They'll be there, no matter the weather. Holding signs, different from week to week, their message for peace prevails. This quiet, constant vigil makes me feel good about our town. I stood with them for a few minutes and the number of people who slowed down to wave or honk amazed me.

110 CORNELL CINEMA

Let's Go Out to the Movies

Cornell Cinema is like a year-round film festival. It has been cited as one of the best campus film exhibition programs in the country, screening close to 150 different films/videos each year, five nights a week, in the beautiful Willard Straight Theatre. They will deepen your love and knowledge of movies. (See entry 287.)

111 SARAH'S PATISSERIE

Get a Sweet Treat

Sarah's Patisserie's pastry and chocolates are so good, they should be illegal. Choose from a dazzling case filled with imaginative chocolates with flavors such as key lime, chili, lemon lavender, or salted honey pecan butter crunch. Freshly baked croissants, cookies, macaroons, and cakes. Saturday is brioche day. Don't miss the made-from-scratch hot chocolate. Love, love, love!

112 DISCOVER THE SIM REDMOND BAND

One of Ithaca's All-Time Favorites

The Sim Redmond Band plays music that is pure joy, an airy, bouncing roots/Afro-Carribean/reggae music that comes together in a dreamy sound. Uniit Carruyo's angelic voice harmonizes perfectly with Sim Redmond's earthy tenor. They have released several fine albums including *Life is Water* and *Good Thoughts* and have played with the likes of the Neville Brothers, the Wailers, and Jimmy Cliff.

113 THE CLINTON HOUSE

A Grand Greek Revival

The Clinton House opened its doors in 1830 and was the grandest hotel west of New York City. At least four US presidents stayed in its rooms. In 1902, the upper two stories were completely gutted in a fire. By 1972, the Clinton House was very run down and in danger of being demolished. Historic Ithaca purchased it and with a small army of volunteers and paid workers rescued the building, and it has been listed on the National Register of Historic Places. Today it houses professional offices and a school. This cherished landmark will now stand for the next 100 years and hopefully beyond. (See entry 160.)

114 ALISON LURIE

Foreign Affairs Is a Must-Read

When Pulitzer Prize–winning author Alison Lurie turned 60, she jubilantly got rid of half her wardrobe, stopped coloring her hair, and gave up wearing makeup. Often called the Jane Austen of contemporary American fiction, she is now 90 years old and still going strong. Many of her comic and satiric novels are set in a fictional college town, "Corinth University," a stand-in for Cornell, where she taught for three decades. Recommended reading: *Foreign Affairs* (the Pulitzer winner), *Truth or Consequences*, or *War Between the Tates*.

115

THE SCIENCENTER

CLIMB, THINK AND BUILD YOUR WAY THROUGH

If you don't have kids, borrow some and take them to the Sciencenter to explore the decibel-measuring scream box, the endlessly fascinating Rube Goldberg-style kinetic sculpture, the space area, and lots of hands-on activities for all ages. Try solving a criminal case by analyzing the evidence. Touch a living sea star and make a wish. Great outdoor play areas, too.

TIP

Free admission on first Sundays in winter months.

116 COMMUNITY SUPPORTED AGRICULTURE

Join One of Our Local CSAs

Here is Silas Conroy from Crooked Carrot, Ithaca's first Community Supported Kitchen, part of the Full Plate Farm Collective. Their products include the world's best pickles, tomato sauce, applesauce, and more. The organic Full Plate Farm Collective CSA (Community Supported Agriculture) includes Stick and Stone Farm, Three Swallows Farm, and Remembrance Farm and offers more than 450 shares to Ithaca households. Members opt for summer, fall, or winter shares of heirloom tomatoes, greens, cukes, squash, potatoes, strawberries, broccoli, beets, pumpkins, watermelon, spinach, onions, and so much more. Food tastes so much better straight off the farm! Buying shares helps support our local farmers. Join one of more than 40 Tompkins County CSA farms.

117 JUST A TASTE

Try the Tapas

Just a Taste is choice hot spot on downtown's Restaurant Row with more than 40 different types of tapas to choose from. These are delicious small plates, beautifully prepared. The chef uses many ingredients from local farms. Try the deep fried potato wedges with chipotle aioli.

NOTE

No reservations.
Just a sip: include a wine flight with your meal—excellent wine list.

118 MULLESTEIN WINTER GARDEN

Enjoy Vibrant Colors

A gray winter day is prime time to walk through the Mullestein Winter Garden at the Cornell Plantations. The vibrant colors will lift your spirits. Bright orange and red fruits of winterberry, yellow and red branches of scrubby dogwoods and willows, and countless hues of blues and greens of numerous evergreens. You can find every color of the rainbow here. (See entry 263.)

119 WHO IS SIMEON DEWITT?

He Founded Ithaca

Simeon DeWitt founded our town and named it Ithaca after the Greek island of Ithaka, home of the hero Odysseus. DeWitt was the state's surveyor-general and made the first complete map of the Empire State in 1802. He designed much of the layout of downtown Ithaca for public buildings, churches, and schools. Many of these lots continue to serve their original intended use. DeWitt retired here and lived in the Clinton House. He died in 1834. Find his home site on DeWitt Place off E. Buffalo Street.

120 EZRA CORNELL

Forever Changed Ithaca's Destiny

"I would found an institution . . ." Twenty-one-year old Ezra Cornell came to Ithaca in 1828. He worked as a carpenter and as a mechanic. In 1842, he laid telegraph pipe and made his fortune in Western Union. He became friends with Andrew Dickson White when they served together in the New York State Senate. (See entry 121 and 363.) Cornell was a self-made, self-taught entrepreneur. White was a scholar and educator with one of the largest private book collections. Cornell asked his advice on the best use for his money. White told him higher learning was the greatest good. Thus began their shared dream and destiny to form a new university.

121 ANDREW DICKSON WHITE

Cornell University's First President

"High above Cayuga's waters . . ." There would be no Cornell University without Andrew Dickson White. It was his eloquence and grand plan: There should be a new university, open to any person. (See entry 120 and 363.) In 1865, they began building it on Ezra Cornell's 300-acre farm on East Hill. Three years later, White was inaugurated as the first president on the Arts Quad, which was still a cow pasture with just one building almost completed. Together, A. D. White and Ezra Cornell created one of the finest universities in the world.

122 ADAM PERL

Stop In to See Him at Pastimes

One of Ithaca's notable figures is Adam Perl, owner of Pastimes, a delightful little antique shop in Dewitt Mall. Adam is a creator of crossword puzzles for the *New York Times*. He also has a wonderful tenor voice and is a charter member of the Ithaca Community Chorus. I love going into Pastimes—they have lots of inexpensive old treasures. It's fun to look through the vintage jewelry, political buttons, old postcards, tintypes, silverware, antique keys, and more.

123 OPERA ITHACA

See Opera Again for the First Time

Opera Ithaca produces traditional, contemporary, and new operas in English so they're accessible to all audiences. They recently hosted a world premiere of *Billy Blythe*, a modern folk opera about a teenaged Bill Clinton that played to full houses. Opera Ithaca is redefining our perception of what opera is all about. When you go to their operas, the music starts, and it doesn't let you go until the very end. See what happens when all that lush beauty catches you by surprise.

124 MYER FARM DISTILLERS

Take a Drive Out Route 89

Stop in at award-winning Myer Farm Distillers in Ovid, New York. At 90 proof, the spirit will warm the soul and widen the smile. Artisanal handmade spirits are made from organic grains grown on their 1,000-acre farm. Sample their bourbon and rye whiskeys, ginger and coffee-flavored vodkas, and Cayuga Gold barrel-aged gin.

125 ICE SKATING AT CASS PARK

Lace Up Your Skates

There's nothing quite like the feeling of gliding on the ice—it's an essential winter experience. A friendly atmosphere for both kids and adults at all skating levels. Skate rentals and lessons are available.

126 THE GREAT DOWNTOWN ITHACA CHILI COOK-OFF

Taste the Best Bowl of Red

The first chili cook-off was in 1952 at the Texas State Fair. We've been hooked ever since. Who makes the best bowl of red in Ithaca? Find out at the annual Great Downtown Ithaca Chili Cook-Off every February, featuring chili prepared by approximately 30 restaurants as they compete for the titles of Best Meat/Overall Chili, Best Vegetarian, and People's Choice Chili.

127 IMAGINE YOUR SUMMER GARDEN

Order Your Seeds and Dream

In the middle of winter, you'll really miss your garden. Sit by the fire with a cup of tea, look through catalogues, order seeds, and dream. You're not alone. Ithaca is a town of mad gardeners. Winter is also the perfect time to dip into *Cultivating Delight: A Natural History of My Garden*, by Diane Ackerman. She takes you on a tour of her Ithaca backyard in such vivid prose you can practically smell her garden!

128 FOLLOW SVANTE MYRICK

A Leading Light

Elected at age 24, Mayor Svante Myrick is one of the youngest mayors in United States history. He not only walks the walk, he shovels it, too! During a city snow day, Myrick offered to help shovel driveways. "I've got four shovels, three gullible roommates, and a schedule full of canceled meetings," he announced on his Facebook page. "Anyone need a hand?" Myrick spent several hours that day shoveling out driveways, cars, and sidewalks. In addition, he's reorganized the police force and attracted $200 million in new development. An avid walker, he turned his reserved mayoral parking space into a mini-park complete with benches. A Cornell graduate, Myrick has an inspiring back-story, overcoming a difficult childhood that included stints living in shelters and sometimes the family car. Myrick's tenure as mayor has received national attention and it will be interesting to see where this pragmatic progressive goes next.

129 ITHACA COLLEGE MUSIC CONCERTS

Attend Fabulous, Free Performances

Did you know faculty and students of the Ithaca College School of Music perform concerts nearly every day of the school year? More than 350 concerts a year—all free and open to the public. Since it was established in 1892 as a conservatory, the IC School of Music has become known as one of the best in the nation, offering a superb blend of world-class faculty, performance opportunities, and state-of-the-art facilities.

130 MADELINE'S RESTAURANT

When You Want Something Special

When you want a more cosmopolitan atmosphere, go to Madeline's on the Commons, an ideal destination for drinks, dessert, and deep conversation or a festive full-course meal. The menu tilts toward Asian fusion.

WARNING

It's nearly impossible to resist their desserts.

TIP

The bartenders make fabulous martinis and you'll find one of the finest collections of single-malt scotch whiskies in town.

131 FIND THE EIGHT SQUARE SCHOOL HOUSE

Living History

The Eight Square School House is on Upper Hanshaw Road in Dryden. It is the only brick, octagonal, one-room schoolhouse left standing in New York State. Built in 1827, it functioned as a school until 1941 and is now the site of a living history program. Fourth-graders come and experience a typical 1892 school day. Teachers use an authentic 1890s curriculum including pen-and-ink penmanship and reading aloud from primers. Children dress in historical costumes and bring lunches similar to what their great-great-grandparents might have taken to school.

132 CRY BABY CINEMA

Enjoy a Mom's Day Out

Cry Baby Cinema at Cinemapolis features baby-friendly matinees with the volume lower and the lights brighter. No angry "Shhh!" Every Thursday, this special matinee gives new parents a chance to actually watch a movie, in a theater, with their babies. A short reprieve! Doors open at 11 a.m. (See entry 8.)

133 VLADIMIR NABAKOV

Make a Pilgrimage

Vladimir Nabokov wrote *Lolita*, his literary masterpiece, at 802 E. Seneca Street. When Nabokov tried to burn the rough draft, his wife, Vera, changed literary history by rescuing the manuscript from the incinerator. He and Vera lived in nine other rental homes during their time in Ithaca, including 957 E. State Street, 623 Highland Road, 106 Hampton Road, 101 Irving Place, 700 Stewart Avenue, 808 Hanshaw Road, 425 Hanshaw Road, 880 Highland Road, and 404 Highland Road. As profits from *Lolita* multiplied, Nabokov could afford to devote himself wholly to his art. In 1959, he resigned from Cornell to write full time. P.S. We all need a Vera in our lives to save the day!

134 ON THE STREET PITAS

Stop In for a Quick Bite

On the Street Pitas is a much-loved, hole-in-the-wall restaurant. Some of Ithaca's tastiest bites hail from random tiny, divey abodes. You've probably driven past it a million times, wondering what *is* that place? The owner, Brian Horvath, builds the best gyro, chicken pita, and falafel pita. You can also find his food cart on the Commons and at the Ithaca Farmers Market in warm weather. Fresh, fresh, fresh ingredients. Awesome food at an affordable price.

135 CORNELL POLO

Spectators Are Welcome

What to wear to a polo match? There's something impossibly alluring about those mallet-wielding riders wearing white pants and knee-high boots on those beautiful ponies. Cornell women's and men's teams are consistently among the best in the country. The women were national champions in 2015. They play their home matches in the 500-seat indoor arena at the Oxley Equestrian Center. Advice: Don't ask the players if it's like playing croquet on horse

136 GO SNOW SHOEING

Beat the Winter Blahs

I know, I know, you think the snow is never going to melt. After living through more than 35 winters, this southerner can confirm it does go away. So, while it's here, embrace it. Try snowshoeing. It started thousands of years ago as a winter mode of transportation and has now evolved into the ultimate winter workout—you'll burn 600 calories an hour, losing the pounds you gained eating your way through the polar vortex!

137 MARY LORSON

See Her Live Shows

Mary Lorson is one of those songwriters you can put your faith in. She is utterly sublime. Best known for her time as the lead singer of alternative pop group Madder Rose and Saint Low, she is another Ithaca treasure. Currently, she is working on a musical play about Vaudeville star Eva Tanguay. She is also collaborating with author Brian Hall on a British label project, setting a chapter of James Joyce's *Finegan's Wake* to music. She's writing new songs all the time—go see her live shows.

138 WRITE AN INDIGNANT LETTER TO THE EDITOR

In Praise of a Cranky, Dying Art Form

Ithacans are opinionated and articulate. Our local media sources (*Ithaca Journal, Ithaca Times, Ithaca Voice, Cornell Daily Sun*) have lively op-ed pages. Should Cornell pay more for city services? Topics cover politics, fair wages, big-box stores, war and peace, and potholes. And what's with those bridge sculptures, and why is the new Ithaca Commons sign blocked by the traffic light? You'll find the questions and occasional answers here.

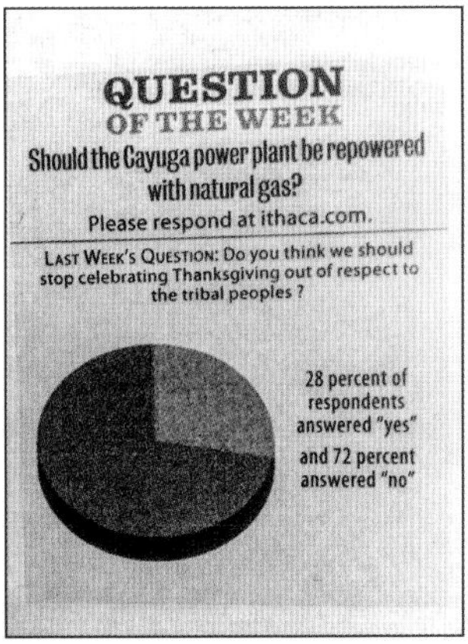

QUESTION OF THE WEEK

Should the Cayuga power plant be repowered with natural gas?

Please respond at ithaca.com.

LAST WEEK'S QUESTION: Do you think we should stop celebrating Thanksgiving out of respect to the tribal peoples ?

28 percent of respondents answered "yes" and 72 percent answered "no"

139 ST. JAMES AME ZION CHURCH

Visit This Stop on the Underground Railroad

St. James AME Zion on Cleveland Avenue is the oldest church in Ithaca, built in 1836. It was the place of worship for free blacks in Tompkins County, and it also was a stop on the Underground Railroad before and during the Civil War. Famous conductor Harriet Tubman visited here. St. James and its congregation continue to be a force for good in our community today.

140 NEW YORK PIZZERIA

Kick Off Pizza Week

Pizza Week! New York Pizzeria in Trumansburg deserves Best in Show and the Best New York-style thin crust pizza. The dough of this hand-tossed pizza is fresh, the sauce is homemade, the cheese is grand, the crust is thin, and it is cooked to perfection. When you walk in the door, stop and inhale the aroma of fresh pizza dough, fresh pizza. It's all they make.

141 SOUVLAKI HOUSE

Go with Greek Pizza

Continue pizza week with the Best New England Greek pizza, at Souvlaki House in Collegetown. Their pizza is hot, fresh, and full of flavor, with generous amounts of garlic. The Popeye Pizza (feta and spinach) is outstanding. Owner Peter Papachryssanthou is a beloved Ithaca institution. For more than 50 years, he has welcomed us into his homey restaurant. He's ageless! Love their Greek salads, garlic breadsticks, and souvlaki, and they have the best spanakopita and moussaka.

142 THE NINES

Move on to Best Deep-Dish

The Nines on College Avenue is as deep-dish as Ithaca gets. The crust is thick and flaky, and the sauce and cheese go on heavy. Order your pie "half cheese" if you worry about your thighs growing. Eclectic toppings. Former Ithacans don't despair: The Nines will ship those square pies anywhere in the US.

TIP

Check out Blue Monday Blues Jam with Pete Panek and the Blue Cats—it's the longest running Blues Jam in the country.

143 COMPARE YOUR WOOD-FIRED PIZZA OPTIONS

Agava and Ithaca Beer

Wood-burning ovens have certainly added fuel to the Ithaca pizza debate—they lift pizzas into another dimension. It's a toss-up. The two best chewy, crispy, and blistered wood-fired pizzas are from Ithaca Beer Company and Agava Restaurant. Both use local sources for their toppings.

144 BOX UP PIZZA WEEK

Napoli's, Sal's, and Italian Carry Out

Who do you call when it's late and you're craving pizza? Let's box up the last slice of pizza week with the three best pizza delivery options: Napoli, Sal's, and Italian Carry Out. They make pizza with a nice homemade flavor, and it arrives hot. How much do you tip the pizza delivery person? Recommended: $3/pie or 15 percent of the total. On a snowy night, throw in an extra $2.

145 AMY DICKINSON

Ask Amy

In Amy Dickinson's best-selling memoir *The Mighty Queens of Freeville*, she wrote, "I come from a family of women who have a lot to say." She meets weekly with her aunts and sisters at Dryden Queen Diner—their "window on the world." Her syndicated column, *Ask Amy*, is read by more than 20 million readers. Her advice is rooted right here, right now. We love you, Amy!

146 SAPSQUATCH SUGARBUSH

Learn How to Tap and Make Maple Syrup

The sap is running! There is no better pulse of the change in the air than the maple season. Before the leaf-out each spring, sugar maples produce a sweet sap that can be made into maple syrup. Sapsquatch Sugarbush in Enfield is a local, 500 tap, family-run business and CSA. Learn the fine art of maple syrup production through their volunteer and work-for-trade opportunities. Sign up for your gallon of maple syrup now—liquid gold.

147 THE AEROPLANE FACTORY

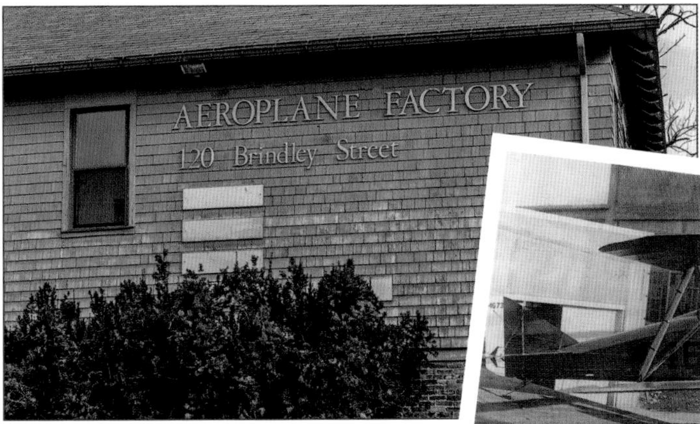

Wings Over Ithaca

During World War I, the Thomas-Morse Aerocraft Company of Ithaca played a pivotal role. Virtually every American combat pilot first soloed in a Thomas-Morse Scout, affectionately known as a "Tommy." The historic aeroplane factory building is still in existence on the West End on Brindley Street. Recently a "Tommy" came home to Ithaca, to be restored to flying condition and preserved as a symbol of Ithaca's aviation history.

148 EMMY'S ORGANICS

Try Their Macaroons and Super Cereals

Emmy's Organics makes guilt-free, gluten-free, vegan, and non-GMO products. They started small at the Ithaca Farmers Market and now their tasty products can be found in thousands of stores nationwide. Created by Ian Gaffney and Samantha Abrams, not-so-typical millennials who provide food made with love in small batches to our community and beyond.

149 ITHACA COLLEGE THEATRE

See a Great Play

Ithaca College Theatre is one of the best theater programs in the country. Their main stage season features plays, musical theater, and opera. Subscriptions are as low as $30 for five shows. Such a deal!

150 CIRCUS CULTURE

Take the Leap

Circus Culture is Ithaca's own circus school. Now you can finally learn the art of trapeze, acrobatics, tight wire, juggling, and more. Founded by Ithaca College alum Amy Cohen, who studied at the San Francisco Circus Center and in London. She's taught circus arts and produced circus events all across the country. Choose from classes, workshops, and camps for adults and kids.

151 WATCH THE LAB OF ORNITHOLOGY'S LIVE BIRD CAM

Nature's Reality Show

A pair of red-tailed hawks, Big Red and Ezra, are nesting in a light tower overlooking Cornell's athletic field. You'll have a bird's-eye view as they prepare their nest, lay eggs, and bring in prey. Watch the eggs hatch, and the babies grow and then learn to fly. Other live Cornell bird cams include the Sapsucker Woods pond cam, barn owls in Texas, and the Laysan albatross in Hawaii.

152 TASTE OF THAI ON THE COMMONS

Explore the Flavors

This is the Thai restaurant favored by Thailand's Princess Bajrakitiyabha Mahidol during her days at Cornell Law School. Authentic, utterly satisfying noodle dishes, satay, curries, and soups. Oh, and they're not afraid to spice things up if you ask.

BEWARE

On a scale from 1 to 10, 3 has kick, 4 will burn, and 5 is hellaciously hot.

153 THE BLIND SPOTS ARE MAKING WAVES

Don't Miss a Chance to Hear Them

This nationally touring Ithaca-based moxy rock band features lead singer and songwriter Maddy Walsh. Her voice is gigantic, and they deliver a high-energy show with uplifting and infectious songs.

154 THE HISTORY CENTER

Unpacking the Past

A visit to the History Center of Tompkins County is like spending time with your favorite relative who knows all the family secrets. Learn everything from the history of Cayuga Lake to stories about the Hungarians and Finns who settled here. Explore unique, rare, and even bizarre objects in their permanent collection. The center has an enthusiastic staff, fascinating exhibits, a research library, and many educational programs.

155 PERFECT HARMONY

Come Sing with Us!

Singing is such a sure-fire way to feel good. We have a plethora of choral groups in Ithaca: Ithaca Community Chorus and Chamber Singers, the Ithaca Gay Men's Choir, the Mostly Motown Chorus, Vitamin L Chorus, the Voices Multicultural Chorus, and the Dorothy Cotton Jubilee Singers. They welcome newcomers to rehearsals, to listen or sing. You don't have to be able to read music or be a great singer to participate.

156 TAKE A HIKE ON THE SOUTH HILL RECREATION WAY

A Scenic Way to Exercise

A popular place to walk/jog is the South Hill Recreation Way. This 3.3-mile gravel path meanders through residential neighborhoods, meadows, and woods, crossing several deep ravines, with views across the Six Mile Creek gorge. It passes through the Mulholland Wildflower Preserve. Hiking paths lead off the biking trail into the gorge.

157 THE KITCHEN THEATRE

Everybody's Talking About It

Go see their latest play! Central New York's off-Broadway theater in Ithaca's lively West End. Subscribe and join the conversations happening in the Kitchen and guarantee yourself multiple evenings of thought-provoking art.

158 PUMPKIN HILL BISTRO

Take a Friend to Lunch

It's a beautiful day to drive out to Pumpkin Hill Bistro for lunch. You'll love the charm of this old farmhouse on 20 acres with views of Cayuga Lake. Comforting food from their open kitchen, like Cookie's Famous Chicken Pot Pie, hits the spot. Just five minutes south of the village of Aurora on Route 90, about 30 minutes from Ithaca.

159 KUMI KORF

Fall in Love with Her Art

Architect, painter, printer, and book artist, the ageless Kumi Korf was born in Japan and has lived for more than fifty years in Ithaca. The two cultures, East and West, can be detected in all her work. Korf is represented in museum collections all over the world.

160 SEE THE MURAL LOUNGE

Inside the Clinton House

In 1948, James O. Mahoney painted this bold and brilliant art deco mural of Ithaca, which gives the lounge its name. On the left are buildings from Cornell's campus and figures representing Cornell student activities, including swimming and crew racing. The central grouping contains characters from mythology headed by Bacchus, god of wine and merriment. A centaur—half man, half horse—and assorted nymphs complete this area. On the right are prominent city buildings, including the Clinton House, and figures suggesting Ithaca College specialties, including drama, music, and photography. Mahoney painted many murals, including one at the 1939 World's Fair. He taught at Cornell School of Architecture. (See entry 113.)

Climb 161 Steps to the Top

You'll have the most magnificent view in all of Ithaca at the top of Cornell's world-famous McGraw Tower, and you'll be on the front row of a chimes master concert. The clock tower is the iconic symbol of Cornell and the heartbeat of campus life. Every Halloween the clock becomes orange glowing jack-o'-lanterns. In March, the clock takes on a greenish hue in anticipation of Dragon Day. (See entry 174.) Trivia: On October 7, 1997, the infamous great pumpkin mysteriously appeared on top of McGraw Tower and endured for most of an Ithaca winter. It remains one of Cornell's most notable pranks. Whodunit? We still don't know. (See entry 290.)

162 GO ON A CIDER SPREE

The Finger Lakes' Next Big Thing

Farmers have been fermenting apples forever, and cider was huge in the US pre-1860. But once Prohibition kicked in, cideries disappeared. We're sure making up for lost time now. Finger Lakes Cider House, Redbyrd Orchard Cider, Bellwether Hard Cider, Black Diamond Cider, Eve's Cidery, and Hazlitt Cider Tree are just some of the many hard ciders available in apple country.

163 LESLYN MCBEAN-CLAIRBORNE

Building Community

Leslyn McBean-Clairborne is a shining light in our community's constellation. She serves on the Tompkins County Legislature and is the director of Greater Ithaca Activities Center (GIAC)—a downtown center for youth and teens. Leslyn does not shy away from tough topics, and she creates solutions that make the community work for everyone. She empowers young people, initiates diverse GIAC programs, and promotes steady race relations. You may not know that Leslyn is also a remarkably gifted actor—now and then you may catch her on the Kitchen Theatre stage.

164 AMERICAN RED CROSS

Give Blood

Did you know the first American Red Cross civilian blood drive in the nation was held in Rochester, New York, in 1948? Following a long winter, blood supplies fall critically low. Give blood. March is Red Cross month.

165 DOUG'S FISH FRY

Sometimes You Have a Craving

Sometimes you crave Doug's Fish Fry. The fish sandwich at this casual place is peerless. A big chunk of fresh haddock encased in a sandy crust with just the right amount of crunchy goodness. Perfect pickle-y tartar sauce and coleslaw with some kick. Crisp fried onion rings or fresh-cut french fries. The two locations, Cortland and Skaneateles, are not far away, but also look for their food truck, which comes regularly to Ithaca.

166 AUGUST MOON SPA

Push the Reset Button

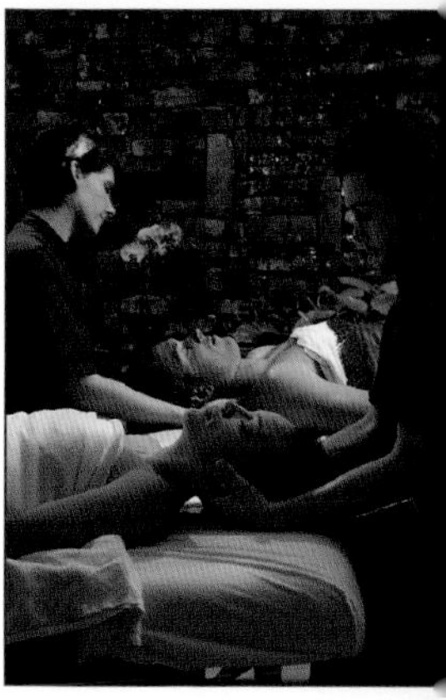

Stop time at August Moon Spa at La Tourelle Resort. Slip into your kimono and relax in one of two Asian-inspired tranquility rooms. Their services include skincare treatments, relaxing massages, and waterfall treatments that will take you somewhere else. Specialty spa packages allow you to try everything including yoga sessions, facials, mudwraps, acupressure, hot stones massage, reflexology, and more. Afterward, enjoy a light, healthy lunch or early dinner at the Bistro.

167 SUBSCRIBE TO THE CORNELL CONCERT SERIES

Bailey Hall

The Cornell Concert Series brings the world's most esteemed performers to Ithaca.

NOTE

Someone once described Bailey Hall as "acoustics by God, seats by Torquemada." A major renovation has remedied the second and improved on the first.

168 WATCH CORNELL AND ITHACA COLLEGE LACROSSE

The Fastest Game on Two Feet

Always popular in the northeast US, it is fast, hard, high-scoring, and fun to watch. Root for the Cornell and Ithaca College teams. It's easy to get hooked. The sport was developed by the Iroquois tribes now of Central New York and played by hunters and warriors to help them train. It was a game they played for the Creator, and it remains sacred to them, almost a religion.

169 ACTING OUT NEW YORK

Sign Your Kid Up for Movie Camp

Looking for a new activity for your kids? Sign them up for movie camp at Acting Out New York. Does your child have a flair for the dramatic? Does he or she need help coming out of his or her shell? It's all about acting out, having fun, building confidence, creative play, and making new friends. Everyone gets a DVD of his or her best work. For kids ages four to 16. Winter break and spring break camp, too.

170 HANG AT THE SHOP

Ideal Place for Getting Work Done

This downtown coffee shop is a cozy place to write or read. Stellar coffee, a welcoming atmosphere, and a tattoo parlor in the back! A whatnow? The bottom line is The Shop is a great place to get some work done.

171 GIVE A SHOUT OUT TO ROBIN SCHWARTZ

Community Arts Partnership

CAP is at the center of arts events that make Ithaca sparkle: Greater Ithaca Art Trail, Spring Writes Literary Festival, the annual Ithaca Artist's Market, and the CAP ArtSpace Gallery. Their primary goal is getting grant funds into the hands of artists and arts organizations. Learn how you can get involved by visiting Robin at the downtown office. (See entry 5, 205, and 288.)

172 SEE THE OLD ITHACA CALENDAR CLOCK BUILDING

Time and Again

Imagine the Calendar Clock building on Dey Street in the 1800s. The Ithaca Calendar Clock Company was widely known for their calendar clocks, which perpetually indicated the month, date, day of the week, and hour of the day. After Prohibition, the company had to close because their business had come from brewers who gave them away as premiums. Today, Ithaca calendar clocks are collectibles—and they still keep perfect time.

173 SIX MILE CREEK VINEYARD

Enjoy a Great Pairing of Wine and Jazz

Beautiful music and view and wine at Six Mile Creek Vineyard, only two miles from downtown Ithaca.

TIP

In addition to red and white wine varieties, they also produce spirits including limoncella, grappa, vodka, and gin.

174 DRAGON DAY

Don't Miss This Colorful Campus Ritual

What the heck is Dragon Day? Dragon Day began in 1901 and is one of the most unique and memorable Cornell traditions. It is a boisterous and colorful rite of spring in March on the last day of classes before spring break. An annual *Revenge of the Nerds* based on the rivalry between the architecture students and engineering students. First-year architecture students build an enormous dragon. Rival engineering students build a phoenix that hovers as the dragon parades by. Campus pranks, thousands of costumed students, and traditions abound.

175 CELEBRATE THE CROCUS

Tiny Pops of Purple Break Through the Snow

Where are the crocuses? Yes! They're here! Go see the brave little crocus blooming. Neither cold nor snow nor ice nor sleet nor more snow nor more cold keeps these little flowers from their appointed round. The Paul Revere of flowers. "Spring is coming! Spring is coming!"

176 COLUMBIA STREET PEDESTRIAN BRIDGE

Take the Shortcut

Walk across the Columbia Street Pedestrian Bridge, and enjoy a spectacular view of Six Mile Creek gorge. This bridge is a great shortcut connecting two hills of Ithaca—stretching from Columbia and Giles Street on South Hill to Ferris Place on East Hill.

177 RACE IN THE ANNUAL SKUNK CABBAGE CLASSIC

Another Harbinger of Spring

The annual Skunk Cabbage Classic Half Marathon and 10k happens every April. This run takes you through Ellis Hollow and features some rolling hills, but most of the route is fast and flat. The famed skunk cabbage can be seen and smelled at the half-way point.

178 THE AMAZING FLAX BARN SALE

Make It an Annual Expedition

Only in Ithaca. The annual Flax Barn Sale happens every April and draws droves of people. Flax Designs began in the 1980s as Angelheart Designs in an old barn. Jeanne Engelhart made funky linen pants, linen tops, and linen dresses. It was a tiny operation, and they sold their clothes out of Handwork in downtown Ithaca. Then one day, Sissy Spacek discovered their clothing. Word spread and suddenly Angelheart Designs was an overnight sensation. Their annual barn sale is an Ithaca tradition and communal experience. Let the clothes buying begin! Here's the thing about pure linen: It wrinkles easily. You can always tell when the sale has happened because the next day, thousands of people are walking around town in baggy, rumpled flax clothing.

179 THE CHAPEL FOR PRAYER AND MEDITATION

Find a New Outlook

Overlooking Ithaca Falls at the end of N. Willard Way is this little spot right on the edge of the gorge that shelters you from rain and quiets racing thoughts. What a view!

180 THE HEIGHTS RESTAURANT AND H BAR

Splurge on a Special Occasion

Birthday. Anniversary. Graduation. Date night. Barely-passed-a-class bash. Celebrate at the Heights Restaurant and H Bar. Exceptional food—the menu is chic and varied—with solid offerings in steak and seafood. Chef James Larounis knows how to present the food with flair so it is visually appealing, and they have inspired appetizers and desserts—definitely get the lava cake.

NOTE

It's pricey but worth it.

181 CONNECTICUT HILL

The High Point in Tompkins County

The highest elevation in Tompkins County is at the top of Connecticut Hill. It is 2,099 feet, and the spot is marked with a stone monument near the Finger Lakes Trail. Open year-round, the Connecticut Hill Wildlife Life Management Area is the largest of its kind in New York State with 11,645 acres—trails abound! Highpointing is an obscure sport of ascending to the point with the highest elevation in a given area. Aficionados work to bag a visit to the highest geographic point in each of the 50 states. Who knew? You may want to take it up. Start slowly with Connecticut Hill, and work your way up. Milestone: You are exactly halfway through the book—the perfect place to note our high point!

182 DRIVE BY THE JOHN J. ELLIS HOUSE

A Silent Sentinel at the Bend in the Road

An elegant Gothic home at 1790 Ellis Hollow Road was built by John J. Ellis in 1840, one of the pioneer families. His father, Peleg, was among the first settlers in the town of Dryden. It stands like a sentinel at the bend in the road and is landmark for all Ithacans. There's just something about it. . . . It is one of two dozen homes in Ellis Hollow that have stood for a century or more.

183

FOLLOW THE SENECA LAKE *Wine Trail*

GO ON A WEEKEND WINE-TASTING JAUNT

Is the grass greener and the water bluer on Seneca Lake? Our sister Finger Lake is stunning, and it's only 40 minutes away. The Seneca Lake Wine Trail is one of the largest—definitely stop in at Bloomer Creek, Lamoreaux Landing, Silver Thread, Standing Stone, Wagner Vineyards, Herman J. Wiemer, Hazlitt, Glenora, and Three Brothers. There are many more award-winning wineries on both sides of the lake along with distilleries, cideries, brewpubs, and restaurants. (See entry 28 and 37.)

184 ITHACA TRIVIA: "PUFF, THE MAGIC DRAGON"

Did You Know It Was Penned in Ithaca?

The lyrics to beloved folk song "Puff, the Magic Dragon" were written by a physics major at Cornell named Leonard Lipton. Legend has it Lipton was meeting a friend one evening for dinner, and he had been thinking about the poem "The Tale of Custard the Dragon." When he got to his friend's house, he wasn't there, so while waiting he used his roommate's typewriter to jot down the words to the poem in his head. He left the poem in the typewriter. Years later, Lipton discovered that the roommate, Peter Yarrow of the folk group Peter, Paul, and Mary, was looking for Lipton so he could give him credit for the lyrics. Lipton still receives royalties from the song.

185 SEEK OUT SIBERIAN SQUILL

Another Early Spring Arrival

A spring event I especially cherish is the blooming Siberian Squill. This tiny flower makes sheets of electric blue in gardens and lawns around Ithaca. It doesn't last long. Look for cobalt blue carpets.

186 AURORA, NY

Take a Look-See Down Main Street

Take a drive to Aurora, New York, for a look-see down Main Street. Population 724. This quaint village on the shore of Cayuga Lake is the home of Wells College. The Fargo Bar & Grill is a popular pub. Have an elegant meal at the 19th-century Aurora Inn or a sandwich at Dorie's Bakery. Shop at the eclectic Mackenzie-Childs or Aurora Shoe Company just down the road.

187 THE ITHACA CHILDREN'S GARDEN

Walk, Climb, Run, and Get Muddy

You won't find another place like it on earth. This three-acre public garden for kids is pure magic. Gaia the giant turtle welcomes you. Walk the labyrinth, pick the flowers, feed the chickens, get muddy, taste an edible plant, and climb a tree. Summer camps and educational programs. Open every day. On the Cayuga Waterfront Trail. Learn more and get involved. (See entry 188.)

188 THE TOUGH TURTLE ADVENTURE OBSTACLE RACE

Challenge Yourself

Slow and steady wins in Ithaca's annual adventure race held in April. A 5k race along the Cayuga Waterfront and Black Diamond Trail with challenging obstacles. Push your body, challenge your wit. You'll climb, sprint, crawl, and slide to the finish. All ages welcome with competitive, general, and family heats. Hundreds of participants raise money to support the Ithaca Children's Garden. Volunteers welcome! (See entry 187.)

189 GO TO CASCADILLA GORGE

Be Renewed

Amid the hustle and bustle is this miracle that takes you away. Walk the Cascadilla Gorge Trail from Linn Street to Collegetown. This dramatic trail ascends 400 feet, and within three minutes, you'll forget you're in downtown Ithaca. The trail was originally built by the Civilian Conservation Corps in the 1930s. During the Great Depression, the CCC also built the network of trails, stonework, overlooks, and bridges in the area state parks.

See Cascadilla Falls Through His Eyes

Many remarkable people have lived in Ithaca, walked these streets, pondered these falls, and gazed at the lake. A. R. Ammons (1926–2001) was one of history's preeminent walking poets. He won the National Book Award for Poetry in 1973 and 1993. Like Walt Whitman before him, Ammons would compose entire poems in his head during his walks. He lived in Ithaca and taught at Cornell. Ammons was the Goldwin Smith Professor of English and Poet in Residence. See Cascadilla Falls through his eyes in his poem.

Cascadilla Falls

I went down by Cascadilla
Falls this
evening, the
stream below the falls,
and picked up a
handsized stone
kidney shaped, testicular, and

thought all its motions into it,
the 800 mph earth spin,
the 190-million-mile yearly
displacement around the sun,
the overriding
grand
haul

of the galaxy with the 30,000
mph of where
the sun's going:
thought all the interweaving
motions
into myself: dropped

the stone to dead rest:
the stream from other motions
broke
rushing over it:
shelterless,
I turned

to the sky and stood still:
Oh
I do
not know where I am going
that I can live my life
by this single creek.

191 GROOVE TO THE GUNPOETS

New School Hip-Hop Sound

The Gunpoets seamlessly fuse hip-hop with pop, rock, funk, and a slew of other genres, drawing massive crowds wherever they go. Holy wow! This Ithaca band is rapidly capturing hearts throughout the region. Catch them live.

192 MIA'S TAPAS BAR AND RESTAURANT

Your New Favorite Place to Go

I love this concept: Asian tapas! This is a must-go for an upscale delicious dinner on the Commons. The menu includes a huge range of choices including gluten-free and vegetarian options.

TIP

The pork buns are dangerously good.

193 SIX MILE CREEK, MULHOLLAND WILDFLOWER PRESERVE AND POTTER'S FALLS.

Take a Hike

Take a hike through Six Mile Creek in the Mulholland Wildflower Preserve, just off Giles Street. This wooded trail—a hop-skip from downtown Ithaca—will take you to Potter's Falls. The first mile of the trail is believed to hold the greatest wildflower diversity in the state.

NOTE

Potter's Falls is known as a skinny-dipping spot. But beware! Swimming is not allowed here.

194 GET SMART YOGURT

The Best Froyo on Planet Ithaca

I'm a little late to the frozen yogurt scene, and I'm hooked. This may be the best frozen yogurt you've ever tasted. Smart Yogurt is locally owned, hip and modern, and made on site with Chobani yogurt. They have a huge variety of super yum flavors to choose from and there is an incredible selection of fresh toppings, too. Very Smart.

195 THE COMMONS MARKET

Step Into the Classic Mom and Pop Store

The tiny Commons Market on North Aurora Street has a surprising variety of goods. For more than 50 years, owner Jim Wells and his dad before him have made it an art form to stock all the things people might want and need. "I have everything but fish sauce," Jim said.

196 TOMPKINS CORTLAND COMMUNITY COLLEGE

Find Your Niche

TC3 continues to evolve and grow. They now operate their own student-run organic farm, supplying fresh farm-to-bistro produce to Coltivare, their downtown culinary center. TC3 offers more than 40 degree programs on their main campus, at the Ithaca and Cortland extension centers, and online. They have a wide variety of online courses including one on writing mystery novels. Check them out, and find your niche.

197 THE SULLIVAN-CLINTON CAMPAIGN

Brought Utter Destruction to the Iroquois

The Sullivan-Clinton Campaign of 1779 was ordered by George Washington to burn out and crush the Iroquois nation. Sullivan's army destroyed more than 50 Iroquois villages. They burned the village of Coreorgonel in what is now Ithaca in September 1779. The village had been occupied by the Tutelo people. Some of Sullivan's men wrote in journals, rhapsodizing about the land they plundered. They described corn "a man on horseback would be hidden in from sight"—corn with 18-foot-high stalks and ears 20 inches long.

198 VISIT GANONDAGAN

The Site of a 17th-Century Seneca Village

The Iroquois called themselves the Haudenosaunee, the People of the Longhouse. The framers of the US Constitution were inspired by their laws and principles. Visit Ganondagan in Victor, just outside Rochester, about an hour and a half from Ithaca. It is the only site in New York State dedicated to Native American history. It was once the main settlement of the Seneca, one of the six nations that made up the Iroquois confederacy. The Seneca refer to Ganondagan as the Place of Peace. It is a fascinating place to learn more about the 2,000 years of Iroquois contributions to art, culture, and society. Tour the full-size replica of a Seneca bark longhouse, and the Seneca Art & Culture Center.

199 HAMMONDSPORT

Getaway to this Keuka Lake Gem

Try the Union Block Italian Bistro for lunch. The Glenn H. Curtiss Aviation Museum is fascinating. Curtiss started with bicycles and ended with airplanes! Visit Bully Hill Vineyards and learn more about its eccentric and colorful founder, Walter S. Taylor. Another major stop on the Keuka Lake Wine Trail is Dr. Konstantin Frank Winery. Dr. Frank was the first to plant *vinifera* grapes from Europe in the Finger Lakes, which forever changed the course of winemaking in the Finger Lakes and the United States. It's an easy hour drive from Ithaca through wine country.

200 FORSYTHIA CITY

Thrill at the Sight

The Wizard of Oz movie starts off in black and white and then switches to color. In Ithaca, we live in black and white during the long winter, but at a certain imperceptible signal, the city is suddenly swathed in flaming yellow banks of forsythia. It's like we switched to full Technicolor—I feel a bit like Dorothy as she walks out her front door into the bursting color of Oz.

NOTE

Before Ithaca was known as "Gorges," it was Forsythia City.

201 DOWNTOWN LIVING TOUR

See Inside Luxury Apartments

Go on the annual Downtown Living Tour, a self-guided tour of unique downtown apartments held in April. You'll tour urban apartments like the newly renovated Apartments Above Homegrown on the Commons, the Lofts@SixMileCreek, Gateway Commons Penthouse, and 140 Seneca Way.

BONUS

Many downtown businesses offer samples and discounts during the tour.

202 PMP—POOR MAN'S PIZZA

Have a Late-Night Nosh at the Hot Truck

If you've ever eaten a Stouffer's french bread pizza, you owe it to the Hot Truck. Founder Bob Petrillose invented the PMP in 1960 and it's said that Stouffer's copied the idea with a frozen imitation. Now try the real thing at the Hot Truck or Shortstop Deli. They range from the basic PMP—bread, sauce, and cheese—to the extravagant Suicide—garlic, sauce, mushrooms, sausage, pepperoni, and mozzarella. Each one is piled with ingredients, then baked open-face.

203 JANE DENNIS

A True Original

Jane Dennis makes sculptural paintings with a mix of materials and moving parts—wood, metal, canvas, and paper. Completely original. One of her sculptures is a permanent installation in the Tompkins County Library. Look for Jane's work at the State of the Art Gallery and online.

204 GROTON, NY

The Typewriter Capital of the World

At one time, the village of Groton was known as the typewriter capital of the world. It's a simple machine, but one that helped launch the country into the information age. Benn Conger founded the Corona Typewriter Company in 1909, which merged in 1926 to form Smith-Corona. The Corona 3 was one of the most successful machines in typewriter history, with more than 600,000 built. In 1983, the Smith-Corona factory closed its doors, and life in Groton changed dramatically. This community of 2,313 people lost a business that had employed 1,200 workers at its peak and brought a measure of hustle and bustle. Groton has survived and evolved as a bedroom community for Ithaca, Cortland, and Syracuse.

205 SPRING WRITES LITERARY FESTIVAL

Spark Your Imagination

Go to the annual Spring Writes Literary Festival and meet the throngs of writers who live in and around Ithaca. Did you know there are so many published authors who live on Tioga Street in Fall Creek they call it Writer's Block? Spring Writes is sponsored by the Community Arts Partnership and held in early spring every year in downtown Ithaca with more than 30 literary-themed events, including workshops, panels, music, discussions, storytelling, fun stuff, and serious stuff.

Spring Writes! LITERARY FESTIVAL

206 VOLUNTEER FOR CORNELL'S DUMP AND RUN EVENT

Recycling on a Grand Scale

Students leaving campus in May donate items they no longer need, and then in August there is a huge sale open to the whole community. A recent Dump and Run collected more than 20 tons of useful items, keeping them out of the landfill, and raised over $60,000 for local charities. There are all sorts of fun volunteer jobs—collecting items in the spring, sorting them in the warehouse during the summer, and working at the sale in August. You'll have a blast.

207 GREGAR BROUS AND VICKI TAYLOR BROUS

Community Champions

Every community has their "doers." Gregar and Vicki quietly say "yes" and help countless local nonprofit organizations as major organizers and hands-on participants. Their fingerprints are on almost every single special event and fundraiser in Ithaca including Ithaca Festival, Grassroots Festival, Apple Harvest Festival, Chili Cook-off, Tough Turtle Adventure Race, AIDS Ride for Life, Downtown Chowder Cook-off and Winter Festival, the Cancer Resource Center Walk-a-thon, the Hospicare Women Swimmin', CSMA Artsbreak, Friends of Stewart Park, Wharton Studios, United Way, Kitchen Theatre, and Hangar Theatre. In addition, they single-handedly saved the annual Community Fireworks. In their spare time, Gregar owns Agava and Rulloff's Restaurant and works at his family's business, Ithaca Bakery and Collegetown Bagels. Vicki has run Brous Consulting, which specializes in marketing, events, and social media. May their example inspire us to chart our own path to do good work, volunteer, and give back.

208 STEWART PARK WILLOWS

Come See Their New Look

Say hello to the Stewart Park Willows sporting their fresh spring green haircuts! (See entry 36).

209 NEW DELHI DIAMONDS

Count On Comfort Food. Indian Style.

New Delhi Diamonds is owned by the Sekhon family, who are originally from Punjab. They have an extensive North Indian menu—open both for lunch and dinner. Their lunch buffet is one of the best deals in town and so good! Many dishes are prepared in a tandoor—a traditional Indian clay oven.

210 DANCE TO THE DESTINATION

An A-List Repertoire

If you hear The Destination is playing, then go. R&B, Latin, swing, funk, and disco. This big nine-piece local dance band is so tight, so good. Three outstanding vocalists, four horns, and an amazing repertoire. You'll dance all night.

211 DELIGHT IN DAFFODILS

Fields of Gold

Finally! Ithaca's procrastinating spring has produced what William Wordsworth would call "a crowd, a host, of golden daffodils."

212 WHAT IS SLOPE DAY?

Cornell's Big Party

Every year, on the last day of class, Cornell hosts a *huuuge* all-day party and concert on Libe Slope—the biggest hill on campus. For Cornell students, it is the best day of the year. For townies, it is a good day to avoid going anywhere near campus.

213 SUFFERJETS! ROLLER DERBY! CASS PARK!

Watch a Roller Derby Bout

It is full-contact, super-fast, filled with bumps and bruises and currently the fastest-growing female sport in America. You can see the SufferJets and the Blue-Stockings play other teams from the region spring, summer, and fall.

TIP

It's often tradition at the end of bouts for spectators to stand around the track and give high-fives to competing skaters. It happens quickly, so jump out of your seat right when the buzzer goes off.

214 FEAST AT THE GREEK FESTIVAL

St. Catherine Greek Orthodox Church

The ladies of St. Catherine Greek Orthodox Church have been cooking up a storm for their annual "Taste of Greece" festival in May. Delicious Greek food and pastries, spanakopita, chicken souvlaki, pastitsio, dolmades, and baklava. While you're there, take a tour of this beautiful historic church.

215 SPRING GARDEN FAIR AND PLANT SALE

See You There

We all go to the annual Spring Garden Fair and Plant Sale organized by the Master Gardener volunteers at Cornell Cooperative Extension. It's held in mid-May at Ithaca High School. You'll find over 40 vendors with a huge variety of annuals, herbs, perennials, and more.

BONUS

You'll get expert gardening advice and plant care tips. Bring plenty of baskets, containers, and wagons to transport your purchases back to the car.

216 HARRIS HILL

Go Soaring

The wind beneath your wings. Flying in a sailplane is probably the closest you'll come to feeling like a bird. Experience silent flight at Harris Hill Gliderport near Elmira, the Soaring Capital of the United States. It's open April through October with public glider rides on weekends. While you're there, stop in at the National Soaring Museum.

217 LANG ELLIOTT

Who Is He and What on Earth Is He Up To?

Lang Elliott brings us the music of nature. A cinematographer, nature sound recordist, author, and speaker, Lang travels all over and records the pristine songs and calls of our native birds, frogs, insects, mammals, and also earth sounds of thunder, wind, and rain. His stunning soundscapes are pure nature recordings and convey exactly what occurred in the wild—there's no mixing or layering. Nature is a potent healing force and you can order selections via digital download or CD.

218 WALK PAST THE MAGNIFICENT SPRAGUE HOUSE

Is It the *Addams Family* House?

There's no question the Sprague House at the corner of South Albany Street and North Titus Avenue strongly resembles the *Addams Family* home! In 1871, Charles Titus built the imposing three-story home for his brother-in-law, Joseph Sprague. For many years, it stood alone on the city block before the tract began to attract builders and residents. It is now a distinctive landmark in the historic Henry St. John neighborhood.

219 WANDER THROUGH THE DEWITT MALL

A Lively Microcosm of Ithaca

In 1971, local architect William Downing purchased this downtown building, rescuing the old Ithaca High School from demolition. His far-reaching vision was to create a European village with a cafe at the center. Bookstores, restaurants, and the coolest mom and pop shops. On the upper floors are unique apartments and offices—there's always a waiting list for these. It's home to the Moosewood restaurant, DeWitt Café, Buffalo Street Books, Cat's Pajamas, Greenstar Oasis, Made in Ithaca, the Bookery, Pastimes, and more.

220 BUSY BEE MARKET

Talk About a Real Find

Busy Bee Market on Cayuga Lake in Interlaken is a seasonal lakeside market and café. Accessible by car, bike, and boat, you'll love this quaint little eatery right on the water. Stop in for a bite and enjoy simple food well prepared and a panoramic lake view. Live music, breakfast and lunch, groceries, produce, and souvenirs. Many natural and organic items and local selections. It's an easy 30-minute drive from Ithaca, or arrive by boat.

221 THE INK SHOP PRINTMAKING CENTER AND OLIVE BRANCH PRESS

See an Exhibit

The Ink Shop is a nonprofit run by artists that promotes fine art prints, works on paper, and artists' books. They curate several exhibitions a year, including group and solo shows and invitationals. The Ink Shop offers workshops in a variety of printmaking and bookmaking techniques. Artists can join the Ink Shop for a reasonable membership fee and gain unlimited access to the studio.

222 ROBERT MOOG

From Trumansburg to Abbey Road

Synthesizer pioneer Robert Moog (rhymes with "vogue") changed music forever. The Moog Synthesizer sparked a revolution in electronic music in the 1960s, and the Beatles, Mick Jagger, and Sun Ra were among the first customers of the then-$11,000 instrument. The original Moog factory was in a storefront on Main Street in Trumansburg. He received his PhD from Cornell in 1965, and died in 2005. The Moog Archive—his notes, plans, drawings, and recordings—are housed in Cornell's Rare and Manuscript Collections.

223

ITHACA BEER COMPANY

SPEND THE AFTERNOON AT THE TAPROOM

Ithaca Beer Company was picked as one of USA Today's 10Best brewpubs in the country and named the #1 Craft Brewery in the state. They brew more than 8,000 gallons of beer a day, and you can watch it happen in their state-of-the-art facility and taproom with industrial decor. Sample 14 of their craft beers on tap including Flower Power and CascaZilla and enjoy their limited menu, which includes wood-fired pizza with fresh toppings and the salty, crispy french fry flight with three sauces. What puts this place over the top is the outdoor dining. Picnic tables, fire pit, bocce court—a fantastic place to enjoy a beer and the sunset.

224 DAVID BORDEN

Shift Gears with His Innovative Music

Listen to the music of David Borden, one of the pioneers of electronic and minimalist music. He has lived in Ithaca since the 1960s and founded the world's first live synthesizer group, Mother Mallard's Portable Masterpiece Co., in 1969 with the generous support of Robert Moog. Their release *Like a Duck to Water* is a marvel of minimalism, space electronics, and contemporary classical. David's *The Continuing Story of Counterpoint* has been called the " 'Goldberg Variations' of minimalism." He composed part of the soundtrack to *The Exorcist* and other films.

225 THE SCENT OF LILACS

In High Bloom

The lilacs put on a show all over Ithaca. In May, the breeze is suddenly full of their heavenly scent. In Celtic culture, the fragrance of the lilac tree was believed to carry humans into fairyland. I believe it.

226 PUDDLEDOCKERS

Cayuga Lake Is Calling Your Name

This summer, spend as much time as you can on the water. Puddledockers on Cayuga Inlet rents/sells kayaks, canoes, and paddle-boards—they offer lessons, too. You might like going on their Cayuga Lake evening paddles or their "celebrate the full moon" paddle.

227 THE HAUNT

Dance All Night

The Haunt has been Ithaca's live music venue since 1969. Check the calendar for shows featuring rock, reggae, funk, soul, jazz, punk, grunge, heavy metal, klezmer, indie rock, swing, and world beat. The nightclub's bar and grill has a menu of burgers, wings, and specialty sandwiches.

228 VOLUNTEER AT THE ITHACA FESTIVAL

You Make It Happen

The Ithaca Festival is our largest annual event, attracting over 30,000 people each year. This nonprofit community arts and music celebration is held the first weekend after Memorial Day, and they need lots of human power to put it on. Grab a friend and take a three-hour shift selling festival buttons and t-shirts together—you'll have a great time. (The sale of these items supports the cost of the event.) There are dozens of volunteer opportunities, including emceeing on one of the stages or helping with the parade. Help make it a great weekend. (See entry 233, 234, 235, and 236.)

229 ANOTHER ROADSIDE ATTRACTION

Grab and Go to a Garage Sale

Yard sale season has begun, blooming like ragweed on lawns across Ithaca. Look for those handmade garage sale signs. Vintage treasures and great deals—it's so much fun to haggle. Never forget the goal: You're in training for The Big Grab—the legendary Route 90 sale, a 50-mile-long garage sale from Montezuma to Homer on the last weekend in July.

230 CORNELL GRADUATION

Pomp and Circumstance

The ringing chimes will give you goosebumps. Somehow it never seems to rain on Cornell graduation. Commencement weekend brings sunny skies and proud parents and family to town. Our population swells to bursting on this weekend—expect long lines of snarled traffic on our narrow streets. The ceremony is held outdoors at the university's Schoellkopf Stadium.

231 CAYUGA WATERFRONT TRAIL

Get Out There

This multi-use trail connects all of Ithaca's most popular waterfront destinations, including Cass Park, Treman Marina and the Ithaca Farmers Market, and allows you to enjoy the waterfront without owning a boat. Walkers, joggers, bicyclists, and inline skaters happily share the 10-foot-wide hard surface. You'll learn a fair amount about Ithaca's waterfront history from interpretive signs along the way. Benches and scenic overlooks make this a special place to relax and exercise.

232 MINOR LEAGUE BASEBALL

Take Me Out to the Ball Game

Abner Doubleday, Auburn, New York, native and Civil War general is apocryphally credited with inventing the game of baseball in Cooperstown, New York. Minor League Baseball is the game distilled—see the baseball stars of tomorrow. The seats are cheap, the food is good, and the creative promotional specials are entertaining. Get out and see the appropriately named Auburn Doubledays, the Binghamton Mets, and the Elmira Pioneers. An easy jaunt—just 30 minutes to Auburn or Elmira, 45 minutes to Binghamton.

233 ITHACA FESTIVAL PARADE

The Parade Is Bigger Than It Looks

The Ithaca Festival parade may just be the best parade you'll ever see. It has a bit of everything including a Volvo Ballet, stilt walkers, giant puppets, the He-Man Chainsaw Marching Band, and more. You'll laugh out loud, hug your neighbor, and be glad you're in Ithaca. We gather in the presence of friends and remind ourselves of the basic goodness that exists in all of us. (See entry 228, 234, 235, and 236.)

234 ITHACA FESTIVAL FOOD

Eat Your Way Through a Food-o-Rama

The food at the Ithaca Festival is a feast of the senses. Dozens of food vendors serve up a wide range of ethnic cuisines. Potato pancakes the size of Frisbees, fresh falafels, roasted corn on the cob, fry bread, BBQ beef, ribs and sandwiches, samosas, pad thai, gyros, curries, and spring rolls. Forget your diets. (See entry 228, 233, 235, and 236.)

235 ITHACA FESTIVAL PERFORMERS

Celebrate the Art Made in Our Own Backyard

The Ithaca Festival showcases the performances of 1,000 local artists—musicians, visual artists, dance and theater troupes, storytellers, community groups, and ensembles. You'll see everyone here from the seven-year old playing in a recorder ensemble to world-renowned musicians who make Ithaca their home. Favorites include Hilby the Skinny German Juggle Boy, Mark Rust, all the belly dance troupes, all the community choruses, The Sim Redmond Band, The Purple Valley, Ithaca Ballet, Samite, The Horseflies, Opera Ithaca, The Gunpoets, The Blind Spots, and so many more! (See entry 228, 233, 234, and 236.)

Find Your Own Magic

The best part of the Ithaca Festival is simply seeing everyone out and about. On a perfect sunny day. Or a rainy one. Relaxed. Having a good time. Indelible little moments. Reminds me of all the reasons I fell in love with Ithaca in the first place. Get out there and find your own festival moments. (See entry 228, 233, 234, and 235.)

237 SIGN UP FOR A YOGA CLASS

Just Keep Breathing

Yoga by definition means "union"—the connection between mind, body, and spirit. Just breathe. Just do it. There are so many excellent yoga studios and teachers in Ithaca; they pop up like mushrooms after a rainstorm. Here are a few: Sunrise Yoga, Blackbird Studio, Ahimsa Yoga, The Yoga School, and Mighty Yoga.

238 ISTANBUL TURKISH KITCHEN

And Now for Something Different

Authentic Turkish cuisine—lamb, beef, and chicken kebabs with just the right marinade and spices. Veggie-rich options. Appetizers like *mucver* (delicate zucchini pancakes) and *sigara borek* (Turkish feta cheese and fresh dill in phyllo dough). Desserts—try the pistachio baklava.

BYOB

Stop off at Red Feet Wine Market on your way.

239 PING-PONG IS BACK

Put Some Spin On It

Ping-pong has finally emerged from the basement and is quickly becoming the pastime of hipsters and the elite alike. Brush up your skills with master player Aziz Kommel in weekly ping-pong matches Sundays at the YMCA. You'll learn quickness, angles, and strategy. All ages and skill levels are welcome. BTW, the YMCA has a great pool, fitness center, swim classes, karate, summer camps, and an outdoor education center.

240 ARCHITECT WILLIAM HENRY MILLER

He Shaped the Look of Ithaca

William Henry Miller came to Ithaca in 1868; he was the first student in the Cornell School of Architecture. After graduating, he stayed in Ithaca and designed over 70 buildings and residences on and off campus. His fingerprints are everywhere, and his signature buildings have shaped Cornell's campus. Get a sense of his style by exploring the Cornell University Library (with the famous McGraw Tower), Barnes Hall, A. D. White House, Risley Hall, Stimson Hall, and the downtown Baptist, Unitarian, and Greek Orthodox churches.

241 LEE GINENTHAL

A Rose by Any Other Name

Lee Ginenthal is the owner of Der Rosenmeister nursery, which is open all summer by appointment. You'll see gorgeous roses trained on every structure imaginable on three acres overlooking the Cayuga Inlet. He has hundreds of varieties. Roses are often considered difficult to grow, but Lee has easy care, disease resistant/no spray, cold hardy roses that will not only survive but flourish in your garden. He also offers workshops, and there is an annual open house.

242 THE ITHACA COMMUNITY ORCHESTRA

Share the Joy of Music Making

The Ithaca Community Orchestra is the musical home of over 40 talented amateur musicians from all walks of life. Under the direction of James Mick, they share quality music with our community, many times in collaboration with other local groups like Ithaca Community Chorus or Opera Ithaca. They give two public concerts a year covering a wide-ranging repertoire, and play in many special events and festivals. They welcome new players—do you have an instrument that's collecting dust but keeps calling you to come back?

243 SEE A SHOW AT THE HANGAR THEATRE

Bravo!

It's time to get your subscription to Hangar Theatre's summer series. This professional, regional theatre features equity actors in award-winning plays and musicals. Come early and enjoy a picnic meal outside, or a snack and drink before the show. The Hangar offers summer main stage productions, summer camps, educational programs for kids, and a full range of other theater activities.

NOTE

The seats are very comfortable.

244 WORKSHOP WEDNESDAYS AT THE JOHNSON MUSEUM OF ART

Create Art in Hands-On Workshops

The Johnson offers weekly drop-in workshops where you can learn to make monotypes, Islamic tiles, sculpt with clay—there is a different media each week. The museum has many other participatory events including Art for Lunch, Sunday Artbreaks, and more.

245 HEAR HANK ROBERTS

Utterly Original Jazz Cellist

Do not miss any opportunity to see Hank Roberts play. This utterly original jazz cellist plays, records, and tours with a number of amazing musicians, including Bill Frisell, one of the greatest jazz guitarists of our time. Roberts and Frisell have been close friends and musical collaborators for 40 years and have performed together in a host of different ensembles.

246 ZIFFY'S LINCOLN STREET DINER

You'll Feel Right at Home

You may have thought diners this classic only existed in the movies. The Lincoln Street Diner is the *Cheers* of Ithaca. There's even a mailman regular at this small, quirky neighborhood place. Get the blueberry pancakes or the Cajun sausage gravy and biscuits. Saturday breakfast is packed, and the waitress is snappy in the best possible way.

247

GO BIKING

BIG HILLS AND FAST DESCENTS IN FINGERLAKIA

The Finger Lakes region is a cycling nirvana. Climb wooded back roads, and visit Treman State Park's 12 waterfalls. Ride to the Ithaca Farmers Market or through Shindagin Hollow State Forest—18 miles of trails cut into 2,000 acres of forest. Or cycle around Cayuga Lake, stopping at 16 sloping vineyards along the way. The Finger Lakes Cycling Club has weekly rides and maps.

248

BUTTERMILK FALLS *State Park*

TREK TO THE HEART OF THE GORGE

Buttermilk Falls State Park: The main waterfall is 165 feet high and the beautiful natural pool at the base is a swimming area. Hike the stairs to the heart of the gorge. Look for Pinnacle Rock—this dramatic 42-foot pillar stands alone in the center of the glen. Listen—water and rock create a deep rumbling sound. A 1.6-mile trail takes you past a series of nine more cascading waterfalls.

249 EAT LUNCH AT CREEKSIDE CAFÉ

Teeny Space, Big Flavor

Folks, there's a teeny tiny place called the Creekside Café in Trumansburg. Open for breakfast and lunch. Seriously decadent, everything made from scratch and locally sourced ingredients. French toast and the best breakfast sandwiches ever, specialty paninis, soups, and amazing desserts.

250 CAYUGA NATURE CENTER

Big Fun for Little Hands

A perfect place for kids to explore, have fun, and learn something, too. Climb an awesome six-story tree house and spend time in the butterfly garden. You can observe and learn from the animals that live on site. There are summer camps and outdoor activities for all ages. This outdoor education center has a spacious lodge on over 200 acres with scenic gorge trails. The Nature Center is part of the Museum of the Earth. (See entry 81.)

251 STRAWBERRIES IN JUNE

Grab a Bucket, Go Picking

Red, ripe, sweet, and juicy. Strawberries are in season during the month of June in the Finger Lakes. Get out there while they last! There are many U-pick farms in the region. Top pick: Silver Queen Farm in Trumansburg.

252 STOP EVERYTHING

It's the First Perfect Day of Summer

The day itself seems to tell you to stop everything and come look closer at the world. A blue-sky day when the air is crisp, the light is shimmering. All of us should listen to that call, because perfect days are like a string of pearls: a perfect treasure.

253 MARK TWAIN

Visit His Study in Elmira

Samuel Clemens was a famous man, but Mark Twain was a superstar. William Faulkner called him the "first truly American writer." He wrote some of his best work in nearby Elmira, including *The Adventures of Tom Sawyer, Adventures of Huckleberry Finn,* and *The Prince and the Pauper*. Make a pilgrimage to Elmira, about 30 miles from downtown Ithaca. It's chock-full of Twain attractions, including his octagonal study and his gravesite. During the months of July and August, Mark Twain trolley tours depart from the Chemung Valley History Museum.

254 TASTE OF THE NATION

Eat. Drink. Give.

Share Our Strength's Taste of the Nation gala night in June gathers dozens of the Ithaca area's best restaurants, chefs, wineries, and breweries, all for the best cause—ending childhood hunger. One hundred percent of the revenue from ticket sales goes to support local anti-hunger organizations.

255

The ITHACA COMMONS

OUR COMMUNITY'S FRONT PORCH

At the heart of Ithaca is a mix of shops with restaurants and some of our most beautiful architectural façades. This is our town's front porch, fostering a sense community and neighborliness. Plenty of comfortable places to sit for a spell, relax, and watch the world go by. This four-block pedestrian center has over 100 shops, restaurants, and street vendors and is where Ithaca's festivals, cook-offs, and summer concert series take place.

256 EAT AT THE RESTAURANT AT ELDERBERRY POND

Best-Kept Secret in Central NY

The Restaurant at Elderberry Pond is the best farm-to-table restaurant in the Finger Lakes. On a 100-acre organic farm in Auburn, it doesn't get any fresher. The salad greens are picked right before the restaurant opens. The food is unbelievably good and features meats from pasture-raised animals and fresh seafood. Elegant dining room. Open seasonally, March through December. About a 30-minute drive from Ithaca.

257 WATERFALL SWIMMING AT LOWER TREMAN

Jump into Summer

This is one of the Weather Channel's top 50 "swimming holes" in the country. A natural swimming pool is located beneath a spectacular waterfall in Lower Treman State Park. It's popular with families for its life-guarded swim area. There are eleven more waterfalls in this park. (See entry 362.)

258 STEVEN STUCKY

A Quiet, Brilliant, American Master

Steven Stucky modestly described himself as a "recovering violist." He was a Pulitzer Prize-winning American composer and taught at Cornell for 34 years. Stucky wrote commissioned works for many of the major American orchestras, including Los Angeles, New York, Philadelphia, and Pittsburgh. For many years, he was the composer-in-residence for the Los Angeles Philharmonic. Two recordings of Stucky's music won Grammy awards: A 1999 recording by the group Chanticleer included his vocal piece, "Cradle Songs," and, in 2008, a recording by pianist Gloria Cheng that included Stucky's solo piano pieces "Four Album Leaves" and "Three Little Variations for David." He died in Ithaca in 2016.

259 FIELDS OF FIREFLIES

Take a Night Walk

Take a night walk just outside the city lights and find a field of fireflies—the first of the season—a mirror to the stars above. In the background, hear a hallelujah chorus of peepers. Magic.

260 CAYUGA LAKE CREAMERY

Are We There Yet?

Ice cream nirvana. Cayuga Lake Creamery has luscious hand-crafted ice cream—no other ice cream will seem as good after you've had theirs. It's hard to choose what to get because there are so many tempting flavors. The sea salt caramel is the perfect blend of salty and sweet. They also have soft-serve frozen custard and soy ice cream. Homemade waffle cones are made on site—absolutely fabulous. In 2010, Cayuga Lake Creamery was voted by *USA Today* as the Top Ice Cream Parlor in New York State. On Route 89 in Interlaken, just about 20 minutes from Ithaca.

261 DOWNTOWN SUMMER CONCERT SERIES

Get Down!

Free live music. Downtown Ithaca's Thursday Night Outdoor Summer Concert Series is outstanding and features some of Ithaca's best musicians. Genres include jazz, blues, reggae, folk, hip-hop, country, bluegrass, rock, and more! Held every week at the Bernie Milton Pavilion on the Commons, June through September.

262 DATE NIGHT AT LE CAFÉ CENT-DIX

C'est magnifique!

This classy little French bistro has delicious food, a great wine list, and a wonderful ambiance. The menu features timeless dishes like steak frites and rotating plats du jour: bouillabaisse on Saturday nights, mussels on Fridays, and more. Enjoy a perfect meal, a perfect evening.

263 SUMMER AT THE CORNELL PLANTATIONS

Walk Through Beauty

You could spend years wandering through the Cornell Plantations and still find something new. This vast living museum is one of Ithaca's greatest treasures. There are botanical gardens, herbs, rhododendrons, and perennials. The 100-acre Newman Arboretum with panoramic views, spectacular gardens, and trees has been ranked #1 as the most beautiful college arboretum. It's a special place to take Hugo for a walk. The Plantations also stewards over 3,400-acres of preserves, including Beebe Lake, Cascadilla Gorge, and Fall Creek. The Nevin Welcome Center has exhibits, lectures, and guided tours. (See entry 118.)

264 VISIT LIVELY RUN GOAT DAIRY

Take a Tour

Lively Run Goat Dairy and their artisanal cheeses have a national reputation for flavor and quality. Take the tour and go behind the scenes and see how their cheese is made and aged. Taste many different varieties of goat and cow cheeses, including their Goat's Milk Feta, Cayuga Blue, Lake Effect Cheddar and Gorge Trail Gouda. Try their famous cheesecake and truffles made with their chèvre. Play with the baby goats in the barn. Lively Run produces over 40,000 pounds of cheese a year and represents the very best in cheese making with happy goats and cows. Located in Interlaken, a 20 minute drive from Ithaca.

265 DRINK PURE ARTESIAN WATER

Land of Good Water

We are blessed to live in the land of good water. Abundant. Clean. Pristine. Slaterville Springs is well known for its artesian wells. One is located in front of the Caroline Town Hall on Route 79, and people come here daily to fill their containers. This tiny spring has been in continuous use since the 1800s and has long been reputed to have magical, healing properties. In 1871, Dr. William Gallagher determined the waters of the "magnetic springs" had curative properties and "spa era" began and lasted through the 1920s. Two hotels opened to accommodate tourists who wanted to take the cure. In 1893, the water from Slaterville Springs won an award at the Columbian Exposition in Chicago for its clarity and excellence.

266 SHORT AND SWEET

Go Cherry Picking

The time has come but it doesn't last long: July is a bowl of cherries. Go at Grisamore Farms in Locke, about 20 minutes from Ithaca. Bring your own containers. They also have buckets you can purchase.

267 SEE FIREWORKS AT STEWART PARK

And the Rockets' Red Glare

As the Fourth of July approaches, make sure you put "see fireworks" on your to-do list. Ithaca Community Fireworks are held at Stewart Park at the water's edge along with live entertainment, food, and kids' activities. Stellar vantage points are all over Ithaca, including Sunset Park. One of my favorite vantage points is on a boat on Cayuga Lake.

268 FUN AT THE FINGER LAKES WINE FESTIVAL

A Showcase of New York Wine and Food

The annual Finger Lakes Wine Festival at the Glen in July gives you the chance to taste wines from over 90 wineries in one fell swoop. Held at the Watkins Glen Racetrack, about thirty minutes from Ithaca, the festival features live music, craft vendors, wine seminars, culinary classes, and cooking demonstrations. Get your tickets early, and stay the whole weekend.

269 MIMI MELEGRITO

Our Beloved Mimi

Mimi Melegrito has touched and changed thousands of lives. Volunteering is part of who she is. When she was a teenager, Mimi emigrated to this country from the Philippines. At age 19, she met Mother Teresa and spent a day with her. "At the time, I didn't know who she was, but I remember how she looked so closely at me and the roughness of her hands." Mimi has a masters of divinity degree and her calling is working with children and seniors. For almost 40 years, she has gone every week to play the piano and have sing-a-longs at area nursing homes and retirement communities—for the Alzheimer's patients, she is a true miracle worker. Before retiring, she led the Ithaca Youth Bureau's One-to-One, Big Brother Big Sister program. Mimi now works with runaway teens. In addition, she remains active in all the Kiwanis service projects and has inspired many others along the way to volunteer. Trust me, when Mimi smiles and asks you to do something, you say yes.

270 KNEE HIGH BY THE FOURTH OF JULY

Watch the Corn Grow

According to an old farming adage, the Fourth of July isn't just our nation's birthday, it's also an important benchmark for your corn crop. If all's going well, it should be "knee-high by the Fourth of July." Here is Hugo checking a cornfield on the Fourth. What's it like near you?

271 GRILL SOME CRISPY CORNELL CHICKEN

Thank You, Bob Baker

A perfect day to fire up the grill. If you like moist, flavorful grilled chicken with golden crispy skin, then of course you'll use the Cornell Chicken BBQ Marinade. It is an upstate New York classic. This time-tested recipe was developed at Cornell by Dr. Bob Baker in the 1950s and is often referred to as "State Fair Chicken." Every Finger Lakes fundraiser, every fire department cookout, every Little League barbecue makes Cornell Chicken. You will fall in love in a hurry with this recipe: 2 cups cider vinegar, 1 cup oil, 1 egg, 3 tablespoons salt, 1 tablespoon poultry seasoning, and black pepper to taste. Blend all ingredients until smooth. Marinate chicken 1–2 hours (overnight is good); baste while cooking. It is the absolute best.

272 HARRIET TUBMAN

Visit Her Home in Auburn

Harriet Tubman was born a slave in 1820 and escaped to freedom in 1849. She recalled later, "When I found I had crossed that line, I looked at my hands to see if I was the same person. There was such a glory over everything; the sun came like gold through the trees, and over the fields, and I felt like I was in Heaven." One of the most remarkable women in American history, Tubman became known as "Moses" for her work as a conductor on the Underground Railroad. Repeatedly she returned to the South and led hundreds of slaves to freedom. "I can say what most conductors can't say—I never ran my train off the track and I never lost a passenger," she said. In 1857, Tubman moved to Auburn, where there was a community of abolitionists and Quakers. Senator William Seward and his wife provided her with a home, which they later sold to her for a small sum. Tubman died in Auburn in 1913.

273 WEED YOUR GARDEN

Stop Procrastinating

This is a chore we want to put off as long as possible. Sometimes it helps to remember how you dreamt of getting your hands in the dirt all winter. Another strategy is to weed a little bit every day. That's not going to happen. A better strategy can be summed up in two words: *mulch instead*!

274 TAUGHANNOCK FALLS STATE PARK SUMMER CONCERT SERIES

Pack a Picnic, Bring Some Friends

A popular summer ritual: Every Saturday evening in July and August, hundreds of people bring picnics, blankets, and lawn chairs and spread out on the broad green lawn overlooking Cayuga Lake. Is there anything better than picnicking with friends on a warm summer night? A fresh crusty loaf of bread, cheeses, various hummus-y dips and wine. And the band begins to play as the day turns to dusk.

275 SEE SHAKESPEARE IN THE PARK

Fun, Bloody Fun!

Every July, the Ithaca Shakespeare Company presents two outdoor shows performed in rotating repertory at Allan H. Treman Marine State Park with Cayuga Lake as their backdrop. Their productions feature Equity and non-Equity actors, with actors and designers coming from central New York, NYC, Chicago, and beyond. There are opportunities to join in the fun as actors and crew, collaborators and volunteers. Thousands attend their shows each season.

| 276 LAURIE CONRAD

The Constant Gardener

Walk through Laurie Conrad's sidewalk gardens in Fall Creek. It is a summer-long fireworks show—as one thing dies out, something new blooms. Always inspiring. Look for the fairy garden and sidewalk chalk. When not gardening, Conrad was a brilliant classical pianist and composer and author of several books. She died in Ithaca in 2016. Her perennial gardens will continue to flourish as her living legacy. You'll find them on Lincoln Street, across from the Fall Creek Laundromat.

| 277 HAVE DINNER AT DAŇO'S HEURIGER ON SENECA LAKE

A Great Break on the Wine Trail

Time your arrival to catch the fiery sunset. Daňo's is a chef-owned, modern restaurant with clean lines, high ceilings, and walls of glass overlooking Seneca Lake. They have a wide-ranging menu that highlights traditional Austrian cuisine—spaetzle, wiener schnitzel, smoked pork chops, and braised cabbage. Heurigers are casual restaurants in and around Vienna. Chef Daňo Hutnik, a former ballet dancer in Vienna, and his wife, Karen Gilman, have transported that experience to the Finger Lakes with house-made smoked meats, local cheeses, and Viennese pastries. The results are as spectacular as the sunsets.

278 WILD BLACKBERRIES

Scramble Through the Hedgerows

Nothing defines summer better than a scramble through a blackberry patch. I can barely fill a bucket because I eat them all on site. Perhaps you will be able to pick enough to make jams, cobbler, or pie. Try to be polite and leave some on the bushes for other people.

279 VISIT FARM SANCTUARY IN WATKINS GLEN

A Place of Compassion

This 175-acre farm is home to over 500 rescued farm animals. The animals love visitors, and you will love spending time with them at this unique shelter. You'll learn about factory farming and see cows, pigs, chickens, turkeys, and other animals experience freedom for the first time in their lives. The sanctuary raises awareness and changes hearts and minds about how our world treats animals.

280 HOMESPUN BOUTIQUE

Knit One. Pearl One.

Take a knitting class with Julie Schroeder at Homespun Boutique in downtown Ithaca. "The great thing about knitting is that it's not a huge investment in equipment," she said. "You can buy a pair of needles for five dollars and a ball of yarn and you're knitting." Her cozy store is filled with luxury yarns plus wools from local farms and stocked with bolts of beautiful fabric. In addition to knitting classes, she solves knitting mysteries. Often folks come into the shop with a project gone wrong, and she will figure out where they went off track.

281

Ithaca BOAT TOURS

SEE CAYUGA LAKE

Cayuga Lake: Would Ithaca be here without it? Now, see it again as if for the first time with Ithaca Boat Tours. They'll give you a glimpse of the human and natural history of the Finger Lakes on their classic six-passenger wooden boat. Tours include Early Bird Picnic Tour, Eco-Tour, Summer Sunset, Farmers Market, and Special Cruise Series.

282 LUDLOWVILLE FALLS

Listen to the Soothing Sound

Ludlowville Falls on Salmon Creek in Lansing is a 35-foot cascade with a massive cave under its caprock. It was used as a backdrop during the silent movie era. You'll find the waterfall in Ludlowville Park, a small tree-lined park.

283 DURAND VAN DOREN

Iron Man

Durand Van Doren has been an artist-blacksmith for over 40 years and is on the Ithaca Art Trail. He has made thousands of pieces. He teaches blacksmithing classes, keeping this vanishing trade alive for the next generation. Durand has been spotlighted in *The New York Times* and has worked with the National Park Service. His work at Cornell University includes the gates at Minns Garden; the large gate at the entrance of Cascadilla Gorge, the lanterns on the front of Willard Straight Hall; and the Moot Court Room at the Law School. Elsewhere, his work is at London's Shakespeare Globe Theatre and the historic Great Camp Sagamore in the Adirondacks, and in many private collections. He works daily at his Mecklenburg forge turning out work from farm repairs to custom home and garden accessories and sculpture.

284 EARTH ARTS

Get in Touch with Nature, the Best Teacher

Earth Arts offers mentoring programs that emphasize learning by connecting children to the natural world. Earth Arts is drinking fresh maple sap on a spring morning, or making lip balm from plants in the summer, or building shelters with forest debris in the fall, or telling stories around a fire in the winter. They have a variety of programs for all ages: summer camps, after school, monthly Saturdays, school break, home school, and preschool.

285 FINGER LAKES COOKING SCHOOL

Learn from One of the Best Chefs in the Region

Award-winning Chef Suzanne Stack, of Suzanne Fine Regional Cuisine in Lodi, has closed her restaurant and opened the Finger Lakes Cooking School. She will offer small classes and demonstrations that focus on appetizer, main dish, and dessert with a variety of cooking techniques. A world-class chef and James Beard semi-finalist, Chef Suzanne said, "You will leave with proven recipes you can count on and, more important, knowledge that you can build on." Pastry chef Anne Robinson will teach various techniques in baking and pastry. The school will take place at Suzanne FRC, a gracious old farmhouse with beautiful views of Seneca Lake about 40 minutes from Ithaca.

286 BLUEBERRIES

Go to Glenhaven Farms

Blueberry pancakes. Blueberry muffins. Fresh blueberries by the handful. U-pick blueberries are ripe July through September. Glenhaven Farm in Trumansburg has 11 acres of blueberries. The length and time of the season varies depending on weather conditions. Pick enough to carry you through the winter. Blueberries are easy to freeze.

287 CORNELL CINEMA UNDER THE STARS

Spend Summer Nights in the Open Air

See classic films outside on the Willard Straight Terrace on select Wednesday evenings. Come early for a view of the sunset over West Hill. Cash bar. Film begins at sunset. (See entry 110.)

288 ITHACA ARTISTS MARKET

Enjoy the Local Color

Local color. Local art. Local food. Local music. The annual Ithaca Artists Market is always in July at the Ithaca Farmers Market. A juried fine art show and sale, open-air marketplace with 70 outstanding artists, food, wine, beer, and jazz. Of course you should have local art hanging in your home. All items are sold by the people who make them. Get to know the artist behind the art.

289 WAFFLE FROLIC

Choose Between Sweet and Savory

"And in the morning, I'm makin' waffles." *Ok, I'm not.* I'm going to Waffle Frolic on the Commons. Fresh waffles—choose from buttermilk, hemp and buckwheat, cornbread, or gluten-free/vegan. Along with butter, powdered sugar, or real maple syrup, you can choose from their toppings, which include lemon curd, fried bananas, Nutella, and beyond. The beyond includes fried chicken and waffles.

FYI

The line is out the door on Saturday and Sunday mornings.

290 REMEMBERING JENNIE MCGRAW-FISKE

Philanthropist and Cornell Benefactor

Jennie McGraw-Fiske was one of the village of Dryden's most notable citizens. Her father, John, was a founding trustee of Cornell. Jennie, a major benefactor like her father, gave Cornell its chime set of nine bells on October 7, 1868, the inauguration day of the university. They were the first chimes to peal over an American campus, and they have rung daily since the university's opening in 1868. In her honor, the clock tower was named McGraw Tower. It is recognized around the world as the symbol of Cornell University. Every morning concert includes a playing of the "Jennie McGraw Rag." She also provided Dryden with its library, the Southworth Library. (See entry 161.)

291 CRAFT BEER

Have an Adventure beyond the Wine Glass

Winemakers have a saying: "It takes a lot of beer to make a good wine." There are now almost 70 breweries and brewpubs in the region, and the number is growing. Upstate New York is the new Pacific Northwest of beer. Explore the Finger Lakes Beer Trail. Cheers!

292

FLAT ROCK

BRING A PICNIC, A BOOK, A KID, AND A DOG

A dreamy, timeless summer day. Fall Creek runs shallow here—it's perfect for wading—and there are giant slabs of shale you can claim as your own private island. I love Flat Rock. So does Hugo. And so will you. Find Flat Rock on Forest Home Drive. Look for the gravel parking area across from the Cornell Plantations (no sign).

293 WIND DOWN CASCADILLA PARK ROAD

The "Crookedest" Street

Drive down Cascadilla Park Road. Actually it's probably safer to walk it. Arts and crafts homes are nestled carefully into the curves, with views onto the gorge and town. Cascadilla Park Road is longer than and rises more than Lombard Street in San Francisco. You wind 270 degrees around houses, potentially coming within inches of them as you navigate the impossible corners. There's not another street like it anywhere else in the world.

294 MARY SHELLEY, FOLK ARTIST

Find Her at the Ithaca Farmers Market

"As an artist, I serve up art, just as a waitress serves up food," says Mary Shelley. "My goal is to produce a quality piece of art that will survive and please long past my lifetime." You can find her carving every summer Saturday at the Ithaca Farmers Market. No one else does work like Mary Shelley. She is a folk artist, a painter, and a woodcarver. Mary has been creating her painted low-relief woodcarvings since 1974. Carved pine, acrylic paint, and gold leaf. Her work is in permanent collections including the Smithsonian, American Folk Art Museum, and Fenimore Art Museum.

295 NATIONAL WOMEN'S HALL OF FAME

Come Stand with Great American Women

The women's rights movement started in Seneca Falls in 1848. Elizabeth Cady Stanton declared voting was a woman's basic right. So much history happened here. Visit the National Women's Hall of Fame and learn the stories of 256 remarkable American women, including Jane Addams, Amelia Earhart, Margaret Mead, Georgia O'Keeffe, and Maya Angelou. Every two years, 10 more distinguished women are inducted into the Hall of Fame during a special ceremony. It is an inspiring place to take your teenaged girls ready to spread their wings. Seneca Falls is about a 40-minute drive from Ithaca.

296 EXPLORE THE BURNED-OVER DISTRICT

The Second Great Awakening

What was it about Western New York in the 1800s that turned ordinary people into mystics and visionaries? The area was known as "The Burned-Over District" for all its religious and social reform including abolition, women's rights, and utopian social experiments. Shakers, Spiritualists, and Mormons originated here. Most amazing is the concentration of key sites—all within a day's drive.

297 SWEET CORN

Straight from the Field

It's here! Get your fill. Remember, sweet corn waits for no one, and it's best eaten the day it's picked. We look forward to this moment all year long. Heaven on earth.

298 WOMEN SWIMMIN'

Take the Plunge

More than 300 women swim 1.2 miles across Cayuga Lake to raise funds for Hospicare and Palliative Services each August. Last year's swim raised over $390,000; 100 percent of the money goes to patient and family care. Speed is not the important thing. It is not a race. Each swimmer gathers financial pledges in honor of someone they loved. The swim takes a lot of fortitude, discipline, and training. You'll be inspired by all the women and their supporters—it is a very moving and empowering day for everyone present. The event is hosted at the Ithaca Yacht Club on Route 89 and more than 200 volunteers ensure that the event remains safe and fun for all. There are always openings for volunteers. Maybe next year you'll swim, too.

299 FINGER LAKES GRASSROOTS FESTIVAL OF MUSIC AND DANCE

Experience the Vibe

You must go to the annual Finger Lakes Grassroots Festival of Music and Dance founded by Donna the Buffalo. This is a phenomenal experience that is like no other. Held in July in Trumansburg Fairgrounds, it's one of the top music festivals in the country, drawing 20,000 visitors. Over 70 hand-picked bands from around the world on four stages, for four days, with the emphasis on world, folk, and ethnic music. Camping is available and many festival-goers pitch tents and stay on site all weekend long. The fairgrounds is transformed into an entire village. The vibe is friendly and relaxed, there's people of all ages and walks of life, and the staff and volunteers keep everything on an even keel. Explore a vast array of wonderful food vendors. There's a huge craft fair. All-night Cajun and zydeco dancing. Kids' activities. Art barn. Healing arts area. Dance workshops. Get your tickets early and bring your dancing shoes (and umbrella). (See entry 58.)

300 THE OLD STONE HEAP

Ithaca's Oldest Home

You've probably seen this home flash past you when you're on Route 96 heading north towards Trumansburg. This historic home is called "Old Stone Heap." It is the oldest continuously inhabited home in Tompkins County. Nathaniel Davenport first arrived in 1791. The present stone house was built in 1820 with a wonderful view of the lake and surrounding hills. It operated as a tavern until 1859. Since then it has been a private family home with many different owners.

301 THE A. D. WHITE READING ROOM

Study in the Hogwarts Library

This reading room in Uris Library at Cornell University might be as close to Hogwarts as you can get. High ceilings, gorgeous wrought iron, and more than a fleeting feeling that if you perused the bookshelves, you'd find a book for Defense Against the Dark Arts. There are three tiers of wrought-iron stacks that house White's diverse 30,000 book collection, as well as his art, artifacts, and furniture.

302 HAZELNUT KITCHEN

Be Daring. Try the Chef's Choice.

The Hazelnut Kitchen in the village of Trumansburg is an excellent restaurant. You'll find fresh, innovative dishes and great wine pairings. Take a chance and try the chef's choice: You place your order and you have no idea what you are getting until it is served. There's a little "bar" at the open kitchen that might be the best seat in the house. Watching the chefs at work is like seeing a ballet performance.

303 FINGER LAKES LAND TRUST

Walk in the Wonderland

Soak up every bit of these long summer days that you possibly can. Walk in the wonderland—the Finger Lakes Land Trust protected lands. Their website includes the entire list of locations along with driving directions. The Finger Lakes Land Trust (FLLT) conserves our region's gorges, forests, lakeshore, and farmland. They also offer nature walks, birdwatching, luncheons, and talks. FLLT is one of our greatest community assets.

304

TAUGHANNOCK *Falls*

A WALK FOR ALL SEASONS

The Gorge Trail is a three-quarter mile walk on a flat, wide trail that ends near the base of Taughannock Falls. This is a pilgrimage that you should make every season. On a hot summer day, your reward is a fine cool mist from the falls and, of course, seeing Taughannock Falls up close. I never get tired of it. I've walked this hundreds of times. Take Route 89 north about eight miles from Ithaca. The parking area for Gorge Trail is on the left. (See entry 23.)

305 ELIZABETH LIVESAY

Shuffle Off to Buffalo

Tap dancing. It makes you smarter, improves your balance, and hey, it's fun making noise! There's something about the sound of taps on a hardwood floor—something about dancing and creating music simultaneously. Elizabeth Livesay has been teaching tap dancing to kids and adults for years at the Community School of Music and Arts. I've taken the class a number of times and love it. See you there! (See entry 91.)

306 PERSEID METEOR SHOWER

See the Shooting Stars

Here come the shooting stars of the Perseid Meteor Shower—a spectacular night show that occurs every year between July 17 and August 24.

BEST BET

Get out to the countryside, away from city lights. Watch the stars. There will be 50 to 100 meteors an hour and most will happen in the dark hours before the dawn.

307 MY TOMATO SANDWICH

It Tastes Like Summer

Take a freshly picked, sun-ripened, locally grown tomato—thickly sliced, sprinkled with salt and pepper, on white bread with mayo. Please do not attempt this with run-of-the-mill supermarket tomatoes. You will be severely disappointed.

308 GO ON THE QUEST

Antiques!

Period furniture, cool retro items, the perfect vintage lamp—the Finger Lakes is a treasure trove for antiques and collectibles. Shop at spots like Mimi's Attic, Found in Ithaca, and Pastimes. Make a day out of it. Go in any direction; the roads are dotted with antique shops. It's a beautiful drive to Penn Yan, Hammondsport, Geneva, or Canandaigua, and each area also has great antique shops to explore.

309 HAMMERSTONE CARPENTRY SCHOOL FOR WOMEN

If I Had a Hammer

Take a class at Hammerstone Carpentry School for Women. How cool is this? This hands-on experience is in a safe, judgment-free environment. It is especially designed for women with little or no carpentry experience, to encourage self-sufficiency. You'll learn the basics, using tiny house construction as the main teaching tool. Classes in timber framing, cider press construction, and furniture making. Sign up for basic Carpentry Skills 101. You go, girl!

310 SALTONSTALL FOUNDATION FOR THE ARTS

Meet the Artists-in-Residence

Come to the open house. Meet the artists-in-residence at the Saltonstall Foundation for the Arts and see their works in progress. Fresh air for New York State poets, writers, photographers, and visual artists. Five artists at a time stay for month-long summer residencies at this beautiful, 200-acre arts colony in Ellis Hollow. The Saltonstall has provided hundreds of New York State artists and writers with space and time to do their work.

311 FOLLOW THE ITHACA-BORN X AMBASSADORS

This Band of Brothers Is Everywhere

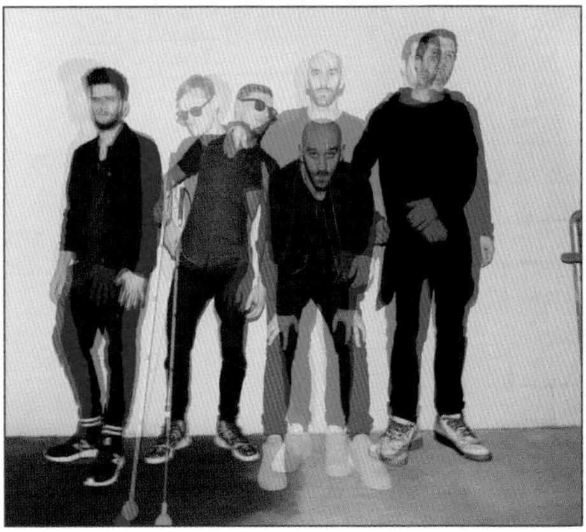

You'll have the X Ambassadors music on repeat. This dynamic, tightly knit indie-rock quartet—Sam (vocals, guitar, saxophone) and Casey Harris (keyboard), plus Noah Feldshuh (guitar) and Adam Levin (drum)—is one of the hottest bands in the country. Their single "Renegades," off their debut studio album *VHS*, rocketed them to number one on alternative radio. This inspirational anthem is a rallying cry for anyone who has defied the odds and it was inspired in part, by keyboardist Harris who has been blind from birth. They started their first band in seventh grade in Ithaca. In 2016, one of their dreams came true: to come back home and sell out the State Theatre. We love the X Ambassadors and are rooting for them to keep writing powerful songs that change hearts and minds.

312 JOHN THOMAS STEAKHOUSE

Enjoy a Sublime Meal

John Thomas is Ithaca's consummate steakhouse featuring dry-aged beef, cooked to perfection, as well as outstanding service and a knowledgeable staff. Heavy sterling and white linens provide a romantic setting. Prices are on par with Ruth's Chris and Morton's steakhouses.

313 THE GLORY OF A SUNFLOWER FIELD

Seek Out This End-of-Summer Vista

In August, sunflowers are at their height. This is the most photogenic flower of all. To truly appreciate the glory of a sunflower field, you have to go in person. Get close enough to see the bees buzzing. Pictured here is one of my favorite fields on Powers Road in King Ferry, with a glimpse of the lake in the background. I go every year, and they nod and bob their heads in greeting.

314 STUDENT ADVISORY

Take Precautions During Student Move-In

A storm of new students with an accompanying flood of parents will hit Ithaca the third week in August. Townies are advised to take the following precautions: 1. Stock up now at Wegmans and Target—those stores will be stripped bare during the storm. 2. If there is anything you need to do in Collegetown or on campus, do it now. 3. Stay off the roads—hazardous driving conditions expected. 4. Do not go out to eat—stay home this weekend.

315 THE TRUMANSBURG FAIR

Have an Old-Fashioned Good Time

The annual Trumansburg Fair in August is a classic country fair with a Ferris wheel, merry-go-round, and other rides. Fair food choices abound. Cotton candy, sausage and peppers, fried dough. Best bets: the demolition derby, fireman's parade, horse show, fireworks, and people-watching! Traditional jams and pie contests.

316 LOOK FOR OLD GREENY

Far Below Cayuga's Waters

Legend has it that Cayuga Lake, one of the deepest lakes in North America, is home to a scaly 15- to 35-foot-long serpentine beast, similar to the Loch Ness Monster. Nicknamed Old Greeny, the first sightings date back to the 1800s. An article printed on January 5, 1897, in the *Ithaca Daily Journal* hails the 69th annual appearance of an elusive green sea monster. The article claims a reputable citizen was taking a drive with a companion along the lake's shore, when he spotted what he said was "certainly the sea serpent" with a large head and long body that disappeared beneath the whitecaps. In 1979, local, professional diver Jack Marshall saw what appeared to be a huge log floating on the surface while boating with friends. They all watched in horror as the mammoth creature submerged before their eyes.

317 JOE CROOKSTON

See Him in Concert

A standout songwriter and magnetic performer, Joe Crookston is beyond good. In 2007, he was awarded a Rockefeller Grant for a project called "Songs of the Finger Lakes." Following in Woody Guthrie's footsteps, he traveled our region for a year collecting stories to turn into songs. His concerts are unforgettable—high energy, rhythmic, lush, and fun. Crookston sings songs that tell a good story and people hoot and holler and listen intently. Crookston was awarded "Album of the Year" in 2009 by the International Folk Alliance.

318 THE CAMP HOUSE IN TRUMANSBURG

Drive by This Stately Mansion

Hermon Camp House is a magnificent federal-style historic home in the village of Trumansburg built by Col. Hermon Camp in 1845–47. Camp was an officer in the War of 1812 and a dominant force in the village. He served as the local postmaster and founded the Tompkins Trust Company in 1836.

319 VISIT THE UNITED LETHARGISTS LEISURE LIBRARY

Little Free Library

"Leave a book, take a book." This Little Free Library on Auburn Street in downtown Ithaca was built as a miniature replica of the main house. Little Free Libraries are a community movement offering free books housed in small containers. "Leave a book, take a book." There are over 30,000 Little Libraries in all 50 United States as well as in 40 other countries. Start your own.

320

Find the GOOD TRUCK

LOCALLY DRIVEN TACOS

Tacos, steak torta, and pozole made with love and fresh local ingredients. Handmade tortillas! Fillings include grilled veggies, coconut black beans, braised brisket, and stewed chicken, and seasonal fillings abound. In addition to weekly and monthly roving locations, The Good Truck offers a variety of catering options.

321 VOLUNTEER FOR THE AIDS RIDE FOR LIFE

100-Mile Bike Ride Around Cayuga Lake

The annual AIDS Ride for Life in September brings together riders, volunteers, and sponsors and helps raise money for the Ithaca/Southern Tier AIDS program. They literally need hundreds of volunteers for the ride to make it happen. Be one of them. Together we can make a world of difference in the lives of people living with HIV/AIDS.

322 NOBEL LAUREATE, HANS BETHE

Strength of Intellect, Strength of Character

His arrival at Cornell as a refugee from Nazi Germany, at age 28 in 1935, launched the physics department into the top echelon. During WWII, Bethe was a key figure on the Manhattan Project. Bethe never regretted his role in the wartime bomb project, for he had feared that Nazi Germany was developing such a weapon; but he was deeply worried by what he had helped to unleash. Soon after 1945, he joined Albert Einstein and others in a public-education campaign. He publicly opposed the development of a hydrogen bomb on moral grounds but participated in its research in the hope that he could prove it impossible. Bethe was awarded the Nobel Prize in 1967 for his work on the stellar energy processes. On the day he learned he had been awarded the Nobel Prize, he still insisted on teaching his regular physics class. Soon after his official retirement, Bethe returned to astrophysics and did cutting-edge research on three different topics until well beyond the age of 90. He died in Ithaca in 2005.

323 THE GREAT NEW YORK STATE FAIR

Plan Your Annual Trek to Syracuse

The Great New York State Fair is in Syracuse at the end of August. A twelve-day kaleidoscopic showcase of all things Empire State. It's a whole lot of contrasts. Thousands of New Yorkers enter competitions spanning arts and crafts, cooking, cattle, agriculture, and more. Culinary offerings present creative ways to have a heart attack. Don't miss the giant butter sculpture and 180-ton sand sculpture. Performances range from Carrie Underwood to old-country party bands and line dancers to regional hypnotist Marshal Manlove.

324 WALK THE SUSPENSION BRIDGE

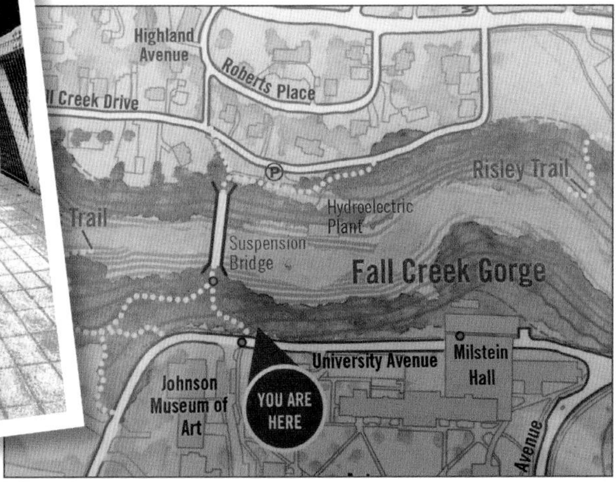

Fall Creek Gorge

Walk across the gently swaying Fall Creek suspension bridge—yes, it does sway even though it looks sturdy—and you'll be rewarded with a spectacular view of Fall Creek Gorge. According to legend, a student crossing the bridge must kiss his or her date or the entire bridge will collapse onto the rocks several hundred feet below.

325 THE ARGOS INN

Have an Elegant Cocktail

This 1831 mansion is a beautifully restored piece of Ithaca history and is now a flourishing 10-room boutique hotel with a public bar and lounge. Head to the zinc-covered bar and try the absinthe and craft cocktails. Bar Argos is a cut above and an inspiring setting for deep conversations. Look for weekly readings, live music, and other special events.

326 PURCHASE PORK TREATS FROM THE PIGGERY

Ithaca's Only Farm-to-Table Butcher Shop

Know your farmer. Know where your food comes from. The Piggery raises heritage pigs on pastures. Their USDA-inspected butcher shop sells handcrafted fresh cuts, specialty sausages, deli meats, and charcuterie. They also offer fresh chicken, beef, and eggs from local, pasture-based farms. Open every day.

327 SHALE

Ithaca's Past Is Written in Stone

Limestone, shale, siltstone, and sandstone. The rocks around Ithaca are cut by thousands of ruler-straight cracks. These natural fractures are called joints. Water flows into the cracks, freezes, and then expands. Eventually, catastrophic failure occurs and a rockslide happens. And so on. During the Ice Age, the gorges were formed by this series of catastrophes. Our lives in Ithaca are shaped similarly.

328 THE GRAND PRIX FESTIVAL OF WATKINS GLEN

Start Your Engines

The Annual Grand Prix Festival of Watkins Glen is held on the Friday after Labor Day. Celebrate the history of the legendary Watkins Glen International with over 100 vintage racecars driving the original 6.6-mile street course to the cheers of 20,000+ spectators.

TIP

While you're there, stop in at Rooster Fish Brewing or the Wildflower Café for a craft brew and a bite to eat. Take a walk through Watkins Glen State Park, which is the most famous of all the Finger Lakes State Parks, with a reputation for leaving visitors spellbound. Watkins Glen is at the base of Seneca Lake, about 30 miles from Ithaca.

329 FIRELIGHT CAMPS

Go Glamping

Unplugged. Natural. Beautiful. Firelight Camps offers fully furnished, luxury safari tents on the forested grounds of La Tourelle and August Moon Spa. At the heart of every great camp is a campfire to forge connections. Guests enjoy a locally sourced breakfast, and can taste local libations during happy hour. Open May through October.

330 CONNIE'S TEX-MEX

Taste Some True Queso

Is there any authentic Tex-Mex in the Finger Lakes? Yes! Connie's in Auburn is the closest I have found. I have no idea what brought Connie from Texas to Auburn—let's hope it was love. Enchiladas, tacos, tamales, nachos, flautas, and burritos. Great combo plates. Jalapeño poppers. Texas red-hot chili and bodacious BBQ. Easy to find—this small but mighty hole-in-the-wall restaurant is next to the maximum-security prison.

331 EXPLORE THE ERIE CANAL

Floating History

The Erie Canal was an audacious idea. Gov. DeWitt Clinton promoted it, and Thomas Jefferson told him to come back in 100 years. They called it "Clinton's Ditch." Built between 1817 and 1825, this 363-mile long canal linked the Atlantic Ocean to the Great Lakes. Before railroads, it brought a flow of people, new ideas, and prosperity. Today, you can boat it, bike the towpath, and explore the locks.

TIP

You can rent a sturdy and comfortable houseboat through Mid-Lakes Navigation Company in Skaneateles and pilot it along the Erie Canal, making stops along the way. *Fun*!

332 CORNELL BIG RED MARCHING BAND

The Band Plays On

I love the Cornell Big Red Marching Band. Full disclosure: I once was a flute-playing, walk-in-step, mouthful of braces band nerd. In addition to seeing them in a sea of red at the stadium, you can catch them drawing a crowd with impromptu concerts—on campus, downtown on the Commons, or at the Ithaca Farmers Market.

333

American Ornithologist and Artist

Louis Agassiz Fuertes was a native Ithacan and the most notable bird artist since Audubon. In 1899, Fuertes accompanied E. H. Harriman on his famous exploration of Alaska. Fuertes traveled across much of the United States and to many countries in pursuit of birds, making thousands of bird paintings. Cornell holds a large collection of his bird illustrations, as well as his personal papers.

In the Presence of Elephants and Whales

Katy Payne is a remarkable Ithacan and acoustic biologist who has listened to the songs of whales and the language of elephants. She was the first to hear and record the songs of the humpback whale. In 1984, she discovered that elephants make infrasonic calls to one another at distances as far as 10 kilometers. Read her compelling book *Silent Thunder*, which tells the story of her discovery. She worked as a researcher in the Bioacoustics Research Program at Cornell's Lab of Ornithology and founded the Elephant Listening Project in 1999. She retired in 2005.

NOTE

Katy Payne is Fuertes's granddaughter—what a great legacy. (See entry 333.)

335 MEGAN SHULL, AWARD-WINNING AUTHOR

Hey, Megan!

Megan is a best selling author and super-sweet, awesome, stupendous human being. Megan has written five books for kids and tweens including *The Swap*, published by HarperCollins—a smart, funny twist on *Freaky Friday*. Ellie and Jack switch bodies through one random wish on the first day of seventh grade. He's her. She's him. *The Swap* is now a Disney Channel Original Movie. Megan has released her next novel, *Bounce*, another hilarious book sure to please your tween.

336 CAYUGA LAKE FLOATING CLASSROOM

Take an Eco-Cruise

Their goal is to get everyone out on the lake. Cayuga Lake Floating Classroom offers public eco-cruises and works with the local schools to get their students on the water in hand-on activities, learning about water quality, plants, fish, and other organisms. The Floating Classroom is available for charter by groups of all ages.

337 ITHACA GUN COMPANY

Annie Get Your Gun

Ithaca Gun Company was founded in 1880 by LeRoy Smith, brother of L. C. Smith (i.e. Smith-Corona typewriters), and W. Henry Baker of Brooktondale, an inventor and gunsmith. They came to Ithaca for its waterpower and set up shop in an old factory near Ithaca Falls. They gained worldwide recognition—Annie Oakley was one of their patrons. For over 100 years they manufactured quality firearms. Their 12-gauge shotguns were the standard used by the LAPD and NYPD. In the 1980s, they had financial difficulties and the original factory in Fall Creek closed. The brick smokestack remains, a remnant of its former glory.

338 SKANEATELES

Absolutely Charming, Full of Sweet Surprises

Jump in the car for a day trip to Skaneateles. You hardly need an excuse to stroll through this village with a European feel at the base of Skaneateles Lake—it's one of the most beautiful of the Finger Lakes. Try great Italian food at Rosalie's Cucina or classic American food at the historic Sherwood Inn. Pamper yourself at the world-class Mirbeau Spa.

NOTE

Pronounce it "skinny-atlas." About an hour's drive from Ithaca.

339 CAMP OUT AT LETCHWORTH STATE PARK

The "Grand Canyon of the East"

This majestic treasure was voted the best state park in the US in 2015. The unforgettable vistas, waterfalls, hiking, hot-air ballooning, and white-water rafting make this a great destination. It is about a two-hour drive from Ithaca.

340 STEP DOWN INTO THE BANDWAGON BREWPUB

Your Downtown Late-Night Spot

Below street level is a friendly place on Cayuga Street with fresh microbrew and locally sourced food. The walls are hewn from a rustic stone. Beer is brewed on the premises, and they also offer flights with beers from elsewhere. If you're looking for a late-night meal, they serve until 1 a.m. Surprisingly varied and delish food. The fries, paired with a flight of beer, paired with a game of darts, equals a great night out.

341 PEDAL AWAY ON A BOXY BIKE

An Electrifying Idea

Boxy Bikes is upstate New York's first electric bike store—they sell and rent custom electric bikes. What a great idea. Car-free living is on the rise in Ithaca. Even our mayor, Svante Myrick, gave up his parking spot at City Hall and walks to work. Boxy Bikes rents all sorts of cool bikes. I have my eye on renting the bicycle built for three.

342 THE BRIDGES OF TOMPKINS COUNTY

Drive Through the Newfield Covered Bridge

The most celebrated is the covered bridge in the village of Newfield—it spans the Cayuga Inlet Creek. Built in 1853 at a cost of $800, it is the oldest covered bridge in New York State that still supports daily traffic. You can see its special construction: uninterrupted criss-cross diagonals called the Town Lattice truss system. The Newfield bridge is the last survivor of the three covered bridges in the county.

343 SEE THE THREE BEARS IN OVID

A Matched Set

There are three Greek Revival brick buildings on the village park in Ovid, New York, which local folks refer to as Papa Bear, Mama Bear, and Baby Bear for obvious reasons. This charming set of historic buildings is unique—there's nothing else like them in the entire United States. An easy 35-minute drive from Ithaca.

344

COUNT DOWN TO *Porchfest*

FALL CREEK NEIGHBORHOOD

Porchfest is one of those brilliant ideas, started by local musicians in 2007, that has now spread to cities across the United States and Canada. Ithaca's Porchfest happens annually on a Sunday in September and the entire Fall Creek neighborhood becomes an open-air music venue for the day. Every year it gets better and better. More than 100 Ithaca musicians take the stage on porches and in front yards, playing blues, reggae, jazz, rock, classical, Latino, hip-hop, and folk, as the audience strolls, bikes, and skateboards through the neighborhood from house to house. I remember seeing a porch filled with a dozen musicians playing only ukuleles! It is a bit surreal, almost like a Fellini movie. You don't know what you'll find around the corner.

345 WHAT'S RIPE NOW?

Indian Creek Farm Will Let You Know

Get on their email list, and you'll be notified when it's time to pick blueberries, cherries, tomatoes, corn, potatoes, onions, garlic, peaches, apples, and pumpkins. During apple harvest season, they have free hayrides and yummy donuts and cider.

346 WALK THE SAGAN PLANET WALK

Billions and Billions

This exact scale model of the solar system was built to honor Cornell Professor Carl Sagan. Although it is a short three-quarter-mile-long walk through Ithaca, it will take you billions and billions of miles across the universe. It is part of the world's largest exhibition, as it extends 5,000 miles to Hawaii with a station depicting Alpha Centari, the star nearest the sun.

NOTE

Carl Sagan was one of Ithaca's most celebrated citizens. (See entry 30.)

347 THE ACETO BROTHERS

Robby. Harry. Eric. Phenomenal. Ithaca. Musicians.

There is an informal rule in Ithaca about live music that at least one Aceto brother must be in the band—part of our local soundtrack for over 40 years. Robby may be the best guitar player you never heard of. On upright and electric bass, banjo, guitar, and mandolin, Harry is one of the busiest musicians in town. Eric is an internationally famous violin builder and plays beautifully on the unique violins he creates in his shop, Ithaca Stringed Instruments. They are pictured here with their father at the 1996 Ithaca Festival.

348 EAT MORE KALE?

Ithaca's Signature Food

This miraculous, trendy, dark leafy green superfood is everywhere—on menus, at potlucks, a giant portion of your CSA share. Kale salad, kale chips, kale smoothies, kale pesto, kale pizza, kale hummus, and kale soup.

349 HEAR THE CAYUGA CHAMBER ORCHESTRA

Ithaca's (Official) Orchestra

You can always count on terrific music from Ithaca's orchestra. The CCO's season begins in September. Conducted by Lanfranco Marcelletti Jr., one of Brazil's most internationally renowned artists. Their concerts, chamber music series, holiday, and special events take place in a variety of great venues. In addition to other programs, they have a successful Youth Outreach Program that visits the schools every spring.

One Perfect Moment

Noted Cornell scientist Carl D. Hopkins happened to notice at a very precise moment that everything comes into alignment. Once a year, on the autumn equinox, at approximately 6:30 p.m., on Cornell's campus in front of Mudd Hall on Tower Road, you can see the sunset flaming through the windows of the Cornell Clock Tower, perfectly aligned. For that one moment: everything is perfect/world peace/I'm OK/You're OK/life is good. Here are Carl and Kathy Hopkins enjoying a CornellHenge perfect moment. Join them next year.

351 CASCADILLA BOAT CLUB

Learn to Row

A familiar sight: college and high-school crew teams rowing up and down the Cayuga Inlet. Rowing looks so graceful when done well—the slim boats glide on the lake like elegant waterbugs. Join them! The Cascadilla Boat Club makes the sport of rowing available to anyone in the community from beginners to masters. Their summer learn-to-row program is based out of their historic boathouse in Stewart Park. You'll be out on the water learning sweep rowing (one oar per rower) and getting a righteous workout across your whole body. (See entry 36.)

352 1960s CORNELL STUDENT PROTESTS

Our Winter of Discontent

Civil rights protests, the antiwar movement, and youth culture transformed Ithaca in the 1960s. It created continual uproar but also a sense that everything was possible. Dozens of communes started. Lavender Hill, Dawes Hill, Yea God, and Fool on the Hill. Many local businesses began in this era based on idealistic principles, such as Moosewood, The Bookery, GreenStar, and Alternatives Federal Credit Union. Grassroots activism remains our legacy.

353 MADE IN ITHACA

Fill Your Home with Functional Art

I drink my morning coffee out of a Frog Hill Pottery mug by Scott Van Gaasbeck. The mug is handmade and wood-fired, dug from his land in Brooktondale. I like knowing it is made from this little patch of earth right here. Explore the hundreds of local artisans and craftspeople making all sorts of functional items—fill your home with beauty and the spirit of Ithaca. Find just the right piece at Ithacamade, Handwork, and the Ithaca Farmers Market.

354 ITHACA CELTIC FESTIVAL

© Dave Burbank

Celebrate Irish and Scottish Culture

Calling all the Clans! Enjoy the annual Ithaca Celtic Festival in October at Stewart Park. Revel in Scottish games, bagpipe bands, sheep shearing, flaming caber toss, Irish step dance classes, Scottish Highland dancing, and athletic competitions. Check out the food and craft vendors and listen to music from Traonach, the Grady Girls, and Doolin O'Dey. Taste some wine from MacGregor Vineyard, or a beer on tap from Bacchus Brewery. Lots of food and craft vendors, too! (See entry 36.)

355 THE TREE CLIMBING INSTITUTE

Go Climb a Tree

I love climbing trees but how do you climb that tree when you can't reach the first branch? Sign up for a course at The Tree Climbing Institute, part of Cornell Outdoor Education. Their tree-climbing courses are for all ages and experience levels, offered in Ithaca and Costa Rica. They also offer a once-in-a-lifetime experience—climbing the world's largest trees, the giant sequoias in California.

356 ENJOY APPLE HARVEST FESTIVAL

A Three-Day Blast on the Commons

The annual Apple Harvest in October transforms the Ithaca Commons with music, food, and family fun at harvest time. Hot apple cider, fresh donuts, and the best kettle corn hit the spot. You'll find varieties of just-picked heirloom apples, monster pumpkins, and more. Amble through dozens of craft vendors. Sample the wares of fabulous local food vendors, wineries, and cideries. You'll have a great time and probably eat too much!

357

THE CARRIAGE HOUSE *Café*

HAVE SUNDAY BRUNCH

Brunch at the Carriage House Café is so good it'll make you cry! The brioche french toast is to die for. Home fries are outstanding and seriously it is the best bacon and sausage ever. They use the finest ingredients and source them locally whenever possible. The breads are baked in-house. All served in a historic, renovated, 1850s two-story carriage house. Voted best brunch in Ithaca by the *Ithaca Times* and the *Cornell Daily Sun*.

Rongovian Embassy to the USA

Alex was an artist, storyteller, chef, generous friend, and ambassador-at-large to the Rongovian Embassy to the USA in Trumansburg—a club he founded in the '70s and known worldwide for great cocktails, zesty Mexican food, live music, and wild shenanigans. Much to his surprise, the Rongo became an institution and has lived on many years beyond Alex. Take note of the huge mural he painted so many years ago depicting the imaginary country of Rongovia—all the place names are the names of his friends. Isn't that what all of us are doing with our lives? Creating countries, whole continents made up of our friends and family.

The Quintessential Ithaca Poem

In the late 1970s, award-winning poet Dick Lourie wrote the quintessential Ithaca poem and later collaborated with local photographer Kathy Morris to create this broadside. It has lived on the fridges of Ithaca for nearly 40 years and perfectly describes small town living. Get your Ithaca poster at Buffalo Street Books.

What It's Like Living In Ithaca New York

here's what it's like: let's say you have just had
lunch someplace in Collegetown and you are
on your way to Karl Jaentsch's garage with
your VW because yesterday
you noticed the brakes were beginning to fade

you start down Buffalo Street hill it
looks like rain now after a sunny morning:
when you slow down for the blinking yellow
light at Stewart Avenue those brakes are
not good

and it gets worse that huge old green
house on the corner of Fountain Place and
then the shiny face of the Terrace Hill Apartments
flash by you like the past you feel terror
in your wrists your stomach and you know
those brakes are gone and you won't be able
to stop at the red light on Aurora

where there are several people leisurely
crossing your path: maybe on their way from
the Unitarian Church to Hal's
Delicatessen or they just left their
own apartment to go buy flowers
or whatever errands we do all day—
in any case there they are and you can't stop

so this is what it's like: as if your brakes
had failed and you couldn't avoid running
right through that crowd knocking them all
apart—
panic broken limbs and screams in the street

well the chances are that on any
given day at least one of these people
would be somebody you had quarreled with
last year and hadn't spoken to since or
a friend you had visited only last week
or even the person you were once married
to yourself
who would see just before the impact that it
was you
that's what it's like living in Ithaca

360 CONCORD GRAPE SEASON

Make Your Own Grape Juice

Late September and early October is Concord grapes season in the Finger Lakes. They are a native crop of the Finger Lakes. Go out to Glendale Farm in Burdett, and pick a bushel to take home and make your own grape juice. If you've never had fresh, homemade grape juice, you are missing out; it's nothing like anything you can buy in a store. It is a magic, revitalizing elixir and will cure what ails you. It's jam-packed with health-protecting antioxidants, as good for the soul as chicken soup, and fun to make.

361 TAKE A FALL DRIVE

Brisk Air. Brilliant Colors.

Mount Pleasant Road is always a source of inspiration. I return here every year and immerse myself in the colors of fall: red, yellow, deep purple, burgundy, gold.

362 WALK THE GORGE TRAIL IN UPPER TREMAN STATE PARK

A Dazzling Fall Walk

In Ithaca, the fall leaves peak around Columbus Day. Upper Treman is the ultimate place to take visitors. It's absolutely breathtaking. Around every corner is something wondrous to see. Twelve waterfalls including the 115-foot Lucifer Falls. If I ever needed a reason to stay in Ithaca, it would be this place. It is quite possibly the best place in the world. (See entry 257.)

363 HAVE YOUR PICTURE TAKEN

While Sitting in A. D. White's Lap

FYI: It's a little tricky getting up there! There would be no Cornell without Andrew Dickson White. Together, he and Ezra Cornell created one of the finest universities in the world, forever changing Ithaca's destiny. Statues of the founders of Cornell are in the Arts Quad on campus. We walk in the footsteps of giants. (See entry 120 and 121.)

364 TAKE FLIGHT IN A HOT-AIR BALLOON

Love Is in the Air

Experience the romance of a hot-air balloon ride. Drift slowly just above the treetops to about 2,000 feet. You can see all of Ithaca; the views are epic. It's so dreamy and quiet. You can plainly hear the sounds of life just below you: people talking and dogs barking. Southern Tier Balloon Rides offers rides about two hours before sunset, taking off from Stewart Park.

All the People You Meet along the Way

The best part of living in Ithaca is the people. They are authentic. No pretense. No dress code. Everyone has a passion—you can't take for granted your first impression. Your real estate agent could be an artist. Your dentist could be a belly dancer. It's a place where you can relax and be yourself. It's not too big, not too small, and chances are good that just around the corner is someone you'll meet who will change your life.

NOTE

This image shows when I first learned how willing Ithacans are to show up and have a bit of fun. In 1991, I had an idea of making an aerial portrait of people spelling out the word Ithaca—a self-portrait of the town if you will. Here we are at Stewart Park, on a Sunday afternoon, at the Ithaca Festival. The letters were marked out on the grass and people filled them in. Photographer Jon Reis was up in a tethered hot-air balloon to get this shot.

Acknowledgments

A special thank you to Cheryl Weber, Catherine Mallette, and the team from Schiffer Publishing, my agent Jill Swenson and editor Jenna Goodman. With a little help from my friends, this love note to Ithaca became so much better. They suggested Ithacacentric things to include and dropped everything to help me find the perfect photographs. With gratitude to Cornell University Photography, Division of Rare and Manuscript Collections at Cornell University, Ithaca College Archives, The History Center, Michael Rider, Diana Drucker, Robyn Wishna, Lisa Smith, Kimberly Hemphill, Debbie Benson, Sarah Hollyday, Perri LoPinto, Jon Reis, Dede Hatch, Dave Burbank, Allison Usavage, Kathy Morris, Mariette Geldenhuys, Laurie Conrad, Fullis Conroy, Dan Smalls, Susie Thurmond, Betsy Gerhardt Pasley, Doug and Shari Schmidt, Dave Davies, Carol Minton Morris, Allen MacNeill, Kathy Hopkins, Marianne Marsh, Mary Fessenden, Judy Barringer, Nancy Zahler, Bill Warren, and the entire cast of thousands of Our Town.

U-PICK
BLUEBERRIES
GLENHAVEN
FARM
WINERY

Index

Index and Contact Information

Photo Credits

All images courtesy the author, with the exception of Ganondagan (public domain) and the following.

Heather Ainsworth; Cogan & Company: Ithaca Community Orchestra, 107
Atlas Bowl: Atlas Bowl, 37
August Moon Spa: August Moon Spa, 76
Judy Barringer: Concord Grape Juice, 162
Barbara Bartholomew: Swimming at Upper Treman, 114
Johanna Brown: Crooked Carrot, 57
Dave Burbank:
Grassroots Festival, 132
The Gunpoets, 87
Ithaca Celtic Festival, 157
Ithaca College Towers, 41
Tommy Burns: The Burns Sisters, 40
George Cannon Images, Running to Places, 37
Carriage House Cafe:
Carriage House Café, 79
Cayuga Chamber Orchestra: Cayuga Chamber Orchestra, 154
Cayuga Nature Center: Cayuga Nature Center, 111
Cinemapolis:
Cinemapolis, 10
Cry Baby Cinema 63
Circus Culture: Circus Culture, 70
The Clay School: The Clay School, 36
Community Arts Parnership:
Greater Ithaca Art Trail, 9
Spring Writes, 91
Ithaca Artists Market, 127
Community School of Music and Art:
Community School of Music and Art, 46
E. Jacob Cornelius:
Corning Museum of Glass, 49
SufferJets, 94
Cornell Cinema: Cornell Cinema, 54
Cornell Tree Climbing Institute: Tree Climbing Institute, 156
Cornell University Department of English: Creative Writing Reading Series, 28
Cornell University Library, Division of Rare and Manuscript Collections:
A.R. Ammons, 86
Ezra Cornell, 58
Louis Agassiz Fuertes, 147
Jennie McGraw-Fiske, 128
Student protests (Courtesy of Alumni Affairs and Development photograph files), 156
Vladimir Nabakov (Photograph by Maclean Dameron), 63
Andrew Dickson White (Photograph by Evan D. Evans), 59
Cornell University Photography:
A. D. White Reading Room, 133
Alison Lurie, 55
Apple Harvest Festival, 158

William Henry Miller, 106
Heights Restaurant and H Bar: Heights Restaurant and H Bar, 82
Jay Hart: Finger Lakes Satellite View, 49
Todd Herron: Trick or Treat in Fall Creek, 16
Gary Hodges Photography:
Sciencenter Building, 56
Sciencenter Exhibit, 56
Carl D. Hopkins: CornellHenge, 155
Wendy Houseworth/Manifesto Designs: Dan Smalls, 15
Ithaca Beer Company:
Ithaca Beer Company, 98
Ithaca Beer Pizza, 67
Ithaca Children's Garden:
Ithaca Children's Garden, 85
Tough Turtle Adventure Obstacle Race, 85
Ithaca College Archives:
Ithaca College Theatre, 70
W. Grant Egbert, 30
Jeff Katsis, Indian Creek Farm, 153
Mike Keenan: David Borden, 99
Kris Krüg, Creative Commons: Katy Payne, 148
Julie Kulik: Earth Arts, 126
Le-Café Cent Dix: Le-Café Cent Dix, 116
Anna Lee: X Ambassadors, 137
Angelo Lisuzzo: Grand Prix Festival, 145
Loaves and Fishes of Tompkins County:
Loaves and Fishes Banner, 51
Loaves and Fishes Volunteers, 51
Rahmel "Ave" Mack: Leslyn McBean-Clairborne, 75
Granger Macy: Cancer Resource Center, 15
Jeff Maggard: Kumi Korf, 73
Rick Manning:
Winter Village Bluegrass Festival, 47
Cayuga Waterfront Trail, 101
Maxie's Supper Club & Oyster Bar: Maxie's Supper Club, 48
Mercato Bar & Kitchen: Mercato Bary & Kitchen, 42
Alice Muhlback: Alice Muhlback, 51
Kathy Morris: What It's Like Living in Ithaca, 161
Museum of the Earth: Museum of the Earth, 41
New York Public Library: Taughannock Falls Walk (Courtesy of Robert N. Dennis collection of stereoscopic views), 134
Northstar House: Northstar House, 35
On the Street Pitas: On the Street Pitas, 64
Opera Ithaca: Opera Ithaca, 59
The Piggery: The Piggery, 144
Ports of NY Winery: Ports of New York, 24
Pumpkin Hill Bistro: Pumpkin Hill Bistro, 73
Rachel Philipson Photography: Hangar Theatre, 107
Racker Centers: Cargill Salt Mine, 45
Rasa Spa: Rasa Spa, 23
Jon Reis:
Ithaca Festival Parade, 102
Ithaca Self-Portrait, 165
K.S. Reynolds: Cayuga Lake Wine Trail, Lucas Vineyards 14
Jane Roberts: Hank Roberts, 108
Darcy Rose: Acting Out New York, 77
David Ruppert: Mulholland Wildflower Preserve, 87
Mark Rust: Hilby the Juggler, Ithaca Festival Performers, 103
Sapsquatch Sugarbush:
Sapsquatch Sugarbush, 68
Tapping Maple Trees, 68
Sarah's Patisserie: Sarah's Patisserie, 54
Doug Schmidt: Snow Shoeing, 64
Shari Schmidt: Cross-Country Skiing, 52
June Seaney: Chandani Belly Dance Troup, 103
Virgil Shields: High Point, 82
The Sim Redmond Band: The Sim Redmond Band, 54
Tony Simons: Firewalker, 11
Six Mile Creek Vineyard: Six Mile Creek Vineyard, 79
Southern Tier AIDS Program: AIDS Ride for Life, 321
Southern Tier Balloons: Hot-Air Balloon, 164

Photo ©Robyn Wishna

LAUREL GUY

Laurel Guy knows Ithaca—its people, landscape, architecture, history, and spirit. She arrived in January 1981, terrified of driving in snow. Once she discovered Smartwool socks, Sorel boots, and all-wheel drive, she never looked back. A founder of the Ithaca Artists Market and Circus Eccentrithaca, she served as director of the Ithaca Festival and the Saltonstall Foundation for the Arts. Guy is a 35-year resident and one of the most successful Realtors in the region. You might find her downtown walking her dog, Hugo, or out in the field making plein-air pastels.

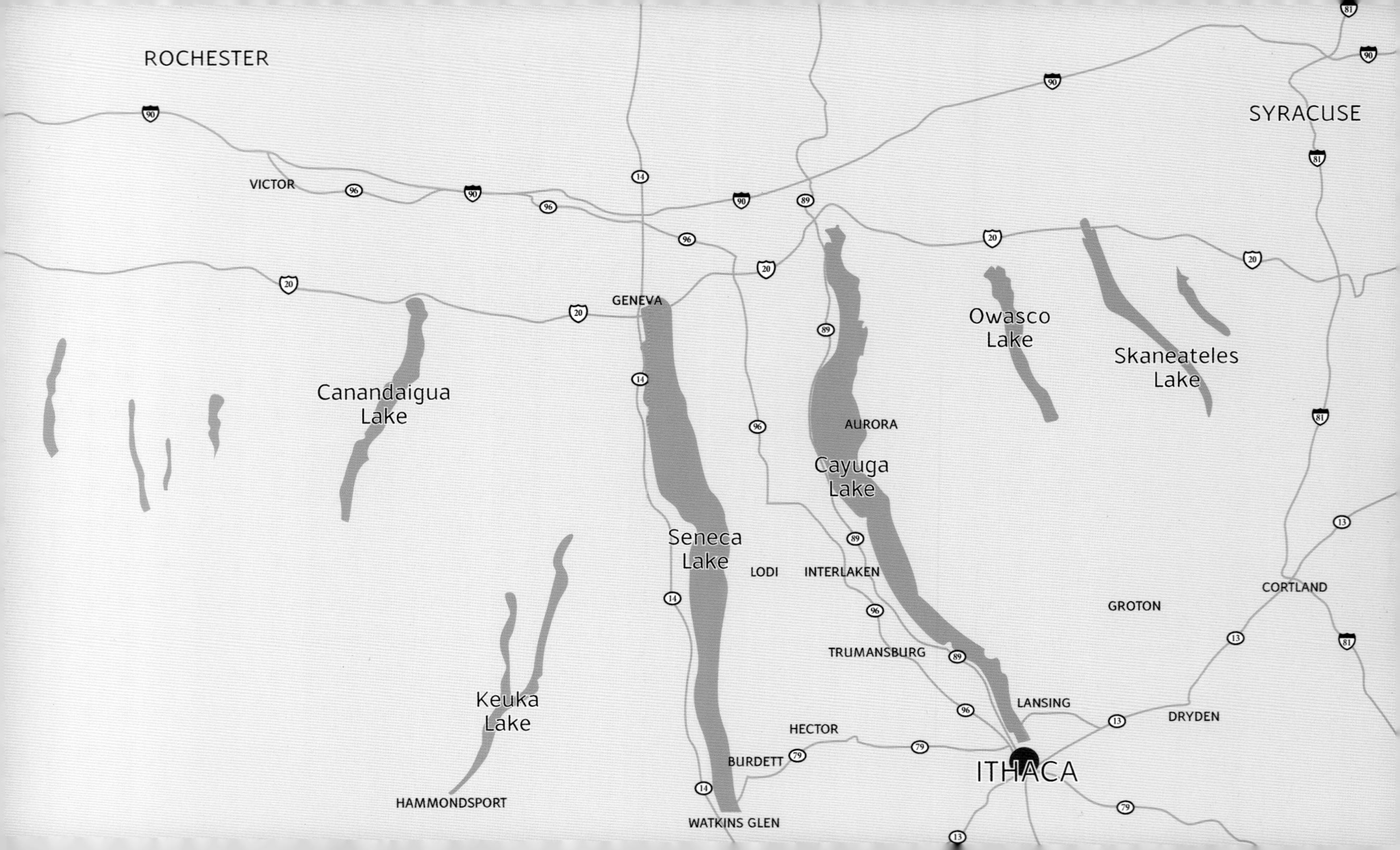
ROCHESTER
SYRACUSE
VICTOR
GENEVA
Canandaigua Lake
Owasco Lake
Skaneateles Lake
AURORA
Cayuga Lake
Seneca Lake
LODI
INTERLAKEN
CORTLAND
GROTON
TRUMANSBURG
Keuka Lake
LANSING
DRYDEN
HECTOR
BURDETT
ITHACA
HAMMONDSPORT
WATKINS GLEN